BLUE EGGS and YELLOW TOMATOES

Recipes from a Modern Kitchen Garden

by Jeanne Kelley

RUNNING PRESS

PHILADELPHIA · LONDON

The publishers would like to express their gratitude to the following people and providers
for their invaluable assistance in the production of this book:

Foster's Homeware (www.ShopFosters.com), Williams Sonoma, Crate and Barrel, and West Elm for providing us with many of the props used in the photographs. A hearty thanks to Charles J. Giunta, Jr., of Giunta's Prime Shop at Reading Terminal Market, for providing us with all of the meats for the shoot. Jim Graham and Stacy Wyn Sarno of Power Plant Productions, LP, for the use of their beautiful studio. Monica Parcell, for her cheerful kitchen assistance. And for his amazing eye and joyfully calm and happy nature, Steve Legato, and his assistant Kerry Angell.

Library of Congress Control Number: 2007929442

ISBN 978-0-7624-3183-0

Cover and interior design by Frances J. Soo Ping Chow
Edited by Diana C. von Glahn
Typography: Abadi, Bembo Titling, ITC Berkeley, P22 Cezanne, and P22 Dearest

Photography by Steve Legato
Photographer's assistant: Kerry Angell
Food styling: Jeanne Kelley
Kitchen assistants: Monica Parcell and Diana C. von Glahn

This book may be ordered by mail from the publisher.
Please include $2.50 for postage and handling.
But try your bookstore first!

Running Press Book Publishers
2300 Chestnut Street
Philadelphia, PA 19103-4371

Visit us on the web!
www.runningpresscooks.com

Contents

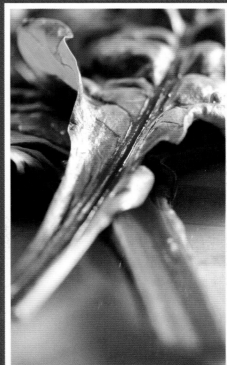

ACKNOWLEDGMENTS

I want to thank my parents, brothers, and sister. Mom, you're a star. You cooked healthy and delicious meals for seven nightly and you always let me make a mess in the kitchen. Pop, your enthusiasm for fine food and good living has been inherited by all your kids who are each in their own right amazing cooks. Matt, your energy and the gusto with which you embrace the cultures and cuisines of all the near and far-flung places you have lived is awesome. Brad, your ability to make fine wine, keep chickens and honey bees, and preserve marmalade, all while working in the world of finance, is inspiring. Jaz, your palate is as finely tuned as the beautiful music you write. Katy, you cook, sew, design, teach, and creatively bring beauty to all aspects of our lives.

I must pay respects to my culinary DNA: to my great-grandparents Reutgen, who owned and ran a bakery in Chino, California, and to my great grandparents Rudolph, who were innkeepers in Valdez, Alaska. To my great-aunts Margaret and Patricia, who were pioneers in the airline food biz (oh, we miss it, now that it's gone), and Auntie Jeanne and the Landis girls, who taught me the joys of (many) freshly baked pies and hand-churned vanilla ice cream.

To Martin, Celeste, and Theresa: I get all sappy just thinking about how I might acknowledge your love and support and numerous talents—words fall short.

I raise a glass to all my friends—you know who you are; you're the ones who share meals with me. What use is good food and drink without the pleasure of your company?

I owe gratitude to *Bon Appetit* magazine—I could practically list the entire staff! But to Barbara Fairchild: Thanks for the opportunity to be part of an excellent magazine; and to Kristine Kidd: it's been so great to work with you on many good stories over the years. Sarah Tenaglia, your friendship, dead-on palate, and perfectionism are inspiring. To Lena Birnbaum, Selma Morrow, Janet McCraken, and Rochelle Palermo Torres, it's a pleasure to cook with you.

Also, I'd like to acknowledge the friendly crew at *Cooking Light* magazine—Mary Kay Culpepper, *et al*: Thanks for letting me contribute to your fine publication.

To Diana von Glahn, my editor at Running Press: Thanks for seeing what this book was really about, guiding me though the process, and offering words of encouragement. I'd also like to thank Frances Soo Ping Chow for her beautiful design sensibility. I'd like to thank my agent, Deborah Ritchken, for her unwavering support and appreciation and knowledge of fine cuisine, and cheers to Karen Kaplan for introducing Deborah to me and singing our praises. A big "merci!" to Monica Parcell, my photo shoot angel. Thank you to Steve Legato and his assistant Kerry Angell for their beautiful work on the studio photography. Also, a tip of the hat goes to Paula Martinet for her excellent assistance and recipe testing.

Blue Eggs and Yellow Tomatoes?

Named for the pretty, pale-blue eggs that my Araucana chickens lay and the juicy yellow heirloom tomatoes that grow in my garden, *Blue Eggs and Yellow Tomatoes* is mostly a collection of good recipes—the kind that I refer to as "keepers"—that you can add to your culinary repertoire and enjoy repeatedly. Many of the recipes are influenced by my travels and my thriving multi-ethnic neighborhood, others by the bounty of beautiful produce at the local farmers' market, and some are simply inspired by what's ripe in my garden. My collection features easy dishes suitable for weeknight suppers, more sophisticated fare for parties, comfort food, snacks, fat sandwiches, good-morning meals, and my favorite desserts.

But there is more to *Blue Eggs and Yellow Tomatoes* than excellent recipes. I include a brief "how-to" for raising a flock of backyard hens, and with the help of my garden-designer husband, provide a simple guide for starting an edible garden. I derive as much joy from collecting freshly laid eggs and picking vine-ripened tomatoes as I do from cooking. Just as I believe in the value of home cooking and the sense of family and tradition it provides, I also love that my family is playing a part, however small, in the food chain. And even though we live in the city, we're connected to the earth and enjoying the healthy process of cultivating nourishment. While I understand that not everyone has the time, space, or inclination to "grow their own," I'm sure you will value the intention and the ingredients that go into these recipes.

Blue Eggs and Yellow Tomatoes attempts to build a bridge between the worlds of convenience and slow foods, between country-fresh and urban-chic. It encourages home cooks to use seasonal and local produce by providing them with healthy, festive, and delicious recipes. In this book, not only do I share my more than 20 years of culinary expertise, I invite you into my kitchen, my garden, and my home. I hope you enjoy them all.

Pantry and Equipment Stocking Guide

A properly stocked pantry is elemental to cooking. When your cupboard holds a wealth of staples, not only is grocery shopping a breeze, but your larder can serve to inspire you to be creative and to cook to your heart's desire. Also, when a well-stocked panty is combined with a vegetable garden, there is always the comfort of knowing that a good dinner can be put together, even if it is something simple like sautéed Swiss chard tossed with pasta and good Parmesan cheese.

. . .

PANTRY BASICS

Salt

I use **kosher salt** for seasoning food before and while cooking. There is something about the texture of the large grains of salt and the way they feel in my hand that allows me to control the amount of salt I add.

I use **fine-grained sea salt** for baking as the larger grains of kosher salt don't always dissolve.

I use **fleur de sel** or other kinds of hand-harvested sea salt to season prepared food just before serving.

Chicken and Beef Broth

Although I sometimes make my own chicken broth from a roast chicken carcass, I never make homemade beef broth or stock. I know purists claim that fresh-made broth and stock are the primary building blocks of cooking—but, to me, it just doesn't jive with home cooking. I like the Better than Bouillon brand bases—they have good flavor, and using them cuts down on cans and cartons as one 8-ounce jar makes 38 cups of broth.

Milk

I prefer organic 2% milk in my coffee and my kids like the reduced-fat milk on their cereal. I don't bother purchasing whole milk for cooking and baking—I use what I have, and that's the 2% milk. Preparing any of the recipes in this book with whole milk is fine, but don't use milk with less than the 2% milkfat as the results may vary.

Essential and Exotic Ingredients

Whenever I use an unusual ingredient in these recipes, I try to provide information about where the ingredient can be purchased. In the lists that follow, I've marked all of the "exotics" with an asterisk. With perhaps the exception of the barberries, all of these ingredients are available online via Amazon.com. Depending on where you live, a mass online pantry shopping spree could save you time and energy. Imagine giving or receiving a copy of this book and a box of the gourmet pantry staples as an extravagant yet practical wedding or housewarming gift!

Ingredients listed in blue are items that no kitchen should be without.

Spices and Herbs

Don't keep dried herbs and spices for more than one year—toss them into your compost pile when their flavor begins to fade.

Achiote powder*	Cumin, seeds	Red pepper flakes,
Allspice, whole	and ground	crushed
and ground	Curry powder	Saffron (keep in an
Caraway seeds	Fennel seeds	airtight container in
Cardamom pods	Ginger, ground	the freezer)
Cayenne Pepper	Herbes de Provence	Star Anise
Chili powder, mild ground	Lavender blossoms,	Sumac*
red, such as ancho, Cali-	dried (culinary	Thyme
fornia, or New Mexico*	lavender)*	Turmeric
Cinnamon, sticks	Nutmeg, whole	Vanilla, beans and
and ground	and ground	extract (keep the
Cloves, whole	Oregano, dried	beans in a ziptop bag
and ground	Paprika, sweet	in the refrigerator)
Coriander, whole	and smoked*	
and ground	Peppercorns	

Oils and Vinegars

I keep all my oils, except for the extra virgin and regular olive oil that I use on an almost daily basis, in the refrigerator so they don't go rancid. Store vinegars in the cupboard.

Corn oil	Balsamic vinegar
Grapeseed oil	Red wine vinegar
Olive oil, regular and extra virgin	Rice wine vinegar, seasoned
Peanut oil, roasted	Sherry wine vinegar
Sesame oil, dark	White balsamic vinegar
Walnut oil, toasted	

Canned Goods

Anchovy fillets in olive oil	Salsa verde
Artichoke hearts, marinated	Sweetened condensed milk
Cannellini beans	Tomatoes, 28-ounce cans diced, and
Chipotle chilies in adobo*	14-ounce cans diced with basil,
Coconut milk	oregano, and garlic
Garbanzo beans	Tuna, in olive oil

Hot Sauces and other Condiments

Chipotle hot sauce*	Ketchup	Olivada*
Dijon mustard	Mayonnaise	Picante sauce
Horseradish	Olek sambal*	Sriracha sauce*

Wine and Spirits

Cointreau	Ruby port	Tequila
Brandy, Calvados	Rum, gold and dark	Vermouth, sweet
or Applejack	Sherry, dry	Vodka
Red wine	Sweet wine	White wine, dry

Dried Fruits

I store dried fruit sealed in plastic bags in a drawer in the refrigerator.

Barberries*	Currants	Prunes
Cherries	Dates	Raisins

Nuts

I also keep nuts, well wrapped, in the refrigerator. Freeze nuts that you don't use frequently.

Almonds, raw, sliced	Hazelnuts	Pine nuts
Almonds, toasted	Peanuts, roasted	Pistachios
and salted	Pecans	Walnuts

Beans, Grains, and Pasta

I store the following in my large "pantry drawer." Always have lots of pasta—it keeps up to 6 months, and you always want to have plenty on hand for a quick-fix dinner.

Barley, pearled	Split peas, yellow	Couscous
Black beans		Fettuccine
Farro, pearled*	Flax seeds*	Orzo
Lentils, French	Pepitas*	Penne
Oats, rolled	Sesame seeds	Rice stick noodles*
Polenta		Rigatoni
Rice, long grain	Graham cracker crumbs	Ziti
and arborio	Panko*	

* exotic ingredients

Sugar, Flour, and Other Baking Necessities

I keep most of these ingredients in my "baking drawer." However, I keep cornmeal, buckwheat, and whole wheat flour in ziptop bags in the refrigerator because they seem particularly susceptible to the little moths that lay webby eggs. I store the vital wheat gluten flour in the freezer to keep it fresh.

Confectioners' (powdered) sugar   Active dry yeast
Light brown sugar   Baking powder
Raw sugar   Baking soda
Sugar   Unflavored gelatin

Buckwheat flour   Bittersweet chocolate
Cornmeal   Chocolate chips
Cornstarch
Unbleached all-purpose flour
Vital wheat gluten flour*
White whole wheat flour

Miscellaneous Staples

Better than Bouillon beef base   Peanut butter
Better than Bouillon chicken base   Picholine olives
Capers   Pickles
Clam juice   Pomegranate molasses*
Green olives, pitted and brine cured   Red Thai curry paste*
Honey   Rice paper wrappers (disks)*
Kalamata olives   Rose water*
Membrillo (quince paste)*   Soy sauce
Molasses   Tahini*
Nam pla (Thai fish sauce)*   Tamarind paste*
Orange flower water*

In the Refrigerator

Aside from the obvious—milk, eggs, and unsalted butter—keep a variety of cheeses, such as Gruyère, Parmesan, and feta. Vacuum-sealed cheeses keep a very long time. I also make a point of always having buttermilk (for pancakes and waffles) and cream.

In the Freezer

I'm not much on frozen foods, but I do keep flash-frozen boneless, skinless chicken thighs for quick dinners, blueberries for pancakes, blackberries for pie, left-over chipotle chilies in adobo, and vanilla ice cream in my freezer.

. . .

APPLIANCES

Blenders: Standard and Immersion

Blenders make a very smooth, fine purée—better than food processors. So they're definitely a necessity. If you have the storage space and you like puréed soups as much as I do, a hand-held or immersion blender is a great time-saving device. Instead of transferring solids and broth from the pot to a conventional blender in batches, you can just immerse the blending wand into the soup and blend. Blenders also are a necessity for making ice cream shakes and smoothies.

Food Processor

Food processors are great for making piecrusts, pesto, and drier purées. The slicing and grating attachments come in handy for large jobs. I was given a Panasonic food processor as a wedding present, and it worked like a champ for about 15 years until I finally wore the motor out. I replaced it with a Cuisinart that I picked up at a secondhand store.

Kitchen Scale

While not absolutely necessary, a kitchen scale is a useful tool when determining portion sizes or when recipes call for ingredients listed in weight. The best scales allow you to place a bowl on the scale and reset the weight to zero so you can measure an ingredient in the bowl.

* exotic ingredients

Choose a scale that measures both small (¼- to ½-ounce) and large (more than 10 pounds) amounts. You might also consider purchasing a scale that can measure both American and metric units of weight.

Spice Grinder or Mill

Grinding your own spices allows for the freshest and most aromatic flavors. This is very easy to do nowadays when most spices that we use in their ground state are also sold as whole seeds. I use an electric coffee grinder that I've set aside especially for grinding spices. However, there are many types of grinders and mills available for use with spices at kitchen supply and specialty stores.

Stand Mixer

These are an investment, but they are definitely worth every penny. Cookie dough mixes together instantly with the paddle attachment, even when your butter is colder than room temperature. Because these mixers stand alone, your hands remain free to make other preparations while the mixer beats, stirs, and whips. I've had my KitchenAid mixer for more than 20 years. It's the basic white model, and it's perfect. Many attachments are also available for stand mixers, from grain mills to juicers to pasta makers.

Toaster Oven

I hide my toaster oven in the corner of the kitchen, but that doesn't mean I don't love it. Its mini-oven is great for reheating and baking small things or single servings. It also uses much less energy than my big oven, and it makes things toasty brown and crunchy instead of soft and soggy like a microwave oven.

Waffle Iron

These come in all shapes and sizes. I prefer the classic waffler to the Belgian-style iron. The heart-shaped ones are particularly appealing. Look for a well-seasoned or nonstick iron.

. . .

BAKING PANS AND DISHES

Heavy baking pans and baking sheets don't warp and make baking easier. I prefer the heavy, rimmed aluminum sheet pans sold in restaurant supply stores. The 16 by 12-inch pan (or 18 by 13-inch, depending on how you measure) with 1-inch-high sides is called a *half sheet* in restaurant lingo, because it's half the size of the pans used in commercial ovens. These easy-to-clean, nonwarping pans are multipurpose; you can use them for baking and roasting. Because they are inexpensive, own at least three—they stack for easy storage.

A rimless baking sheet is good for baking crostatas and for using as a giant spatula. Magic Line makes a good one you can find online. I am not a fan of dark-surfaced baking sheets or pans; in my experience, they burn baked goods, and I find that insulated baking sheets with a "pocket" of air bake too slowly and unevenly.

I'm lucky to have inherited my grandmother's aluminum baking pans, made by Wear-ever. Magic Line makes high-quality aluminum baking pans in almost any size that are available at cookware and craft stores.

Some essential baking pans are:
• Three 9-inch round cake pans with 1½- to 2-inch-high sides
• One 9-inch square pan with 1½- to 2-inch-high sides
• One 8- to 9-inch loaf pan

If you really like to bake, you can also stock your kitchen with a 10-inch springform pan, an 11-inch tart pan with a removable bottom, and a muffin tin.

Baking Dishes

There are many oven-proof dishes that look good at the table. I like to bake pies in glass dishes, usually Pyrex, because glass bakes hotter

than metal and because I can peek at the bottom crust through the clear glass to see if it is properly baked. If you like to bake pies, own several of these. Some essential baking dishes include:

- 8-inch square baking dish
- 13 x 9-inch glass or ceramic baking dish (14-inch oval baking dishes generally have the same capacity)
- 15 x 10 x 2-inch glass or ceramic baking dish
- 9-inch glass pie dishes, with 1½-inch sides and a flat ½-inch rim

Cooling racks are also essential for baking.

. . .

KNIVES AND CUTTING BOARDS

Knives are probably the most important and personal equipment in the kitchen. I recommend trying out as many different shapes, brands, styles, and sizes as possible before purchasing. Offer a hand in friends' kitchens and notice what brand knives they use and how well they work for you. At cookware stores, hold candidates in your hand and simulate chopping and slicing motions—if the store will allow it, chop an onion for a real test.

Chopping, slicing, and dicing are major parts of cooking, and with the proper knives, these tasks are simple. The key is to keep your knives sharp—I have mine professionally sharpened. You can find a qualified knife sharpener through a restaurant supply store, some cookware stores, and even some chefs—and then maintain the edge with a steel.

Boning Knife

A boning knife, while not absolutely necessary, can be very useful for deboning chicken and fish.

Chef's Knife

The most important knife and the biggest investment is the chef's knife. This knife is used for chopping, mincing, and slicing. Look for a high-carbon stainless steel blade, because they hold an edge longer and sharpen easily. The knife should "rock" gently on the cutting board when you mince and the handle should feel comfortable in your hand. I prefer an 8- to 9-inch long blade.

Kitchen Shears

Heavy-duty kitchen shears that can cut through a whole chicken and neatly trim your parchment paper are a great investment.

Paring Knife

Small paring knives are ideal for trimming meats, fruits, and vegetables.

Serrated Knife

A long serrated slicing knife is a must for cutting into bread and cooked meats. I have a great restaurant-style 12-inch blade with a white plastic handle that I picked up very inexpensively about 12 years ago.

Medium-sized serrated knives are good for slicing tomatoes.

Slicers

Slicers, such as mandolins and "v" slicers come in handy when a recipe requires thinly slicing large quantities. Stainless steel mandolins are expensive and can be, frankly, pretty scary. I prefer the smaller, hand-held slicers (some have ceramic blades) that you can buy at the supermarket or cookware stores.

Cutting Boards

For chopping fruits and vegetables, I prefer a large butcher-block-style cutting board. I like the way knives feel on wooden boards. They feel safer, as knives tend to slip on hard plastic surfaces. In my kitchen, I reserve one cutting board for chopping onions and garlic and another for preparing fruit. Even a well-cleaned board will transfer oils from onion and garlic onto fruit and impart a bad flavor.

I always use flexible plastic chopping mats or liners on my cutting boards when cutting raw meat, fish, or poultry. The mats are dishwasher safe, lessening the risk of bacterial contamination. They are also convenient, since they can be used to transfer the raw foods, while avoiding contact with your hands. They're also great for chopping chocolate.

I also think a carving board is essential. A two-sided carving board is best: One side should be flat, perfect for pizza, and the other side should have grooves or a reservoir to catch the juices from cooked meat.

. . .

POTS AND PANS

Quality pans have a heavy bottom and sides that distribute heat evenly, without thin "hot spots" that burn. Unless a pot or pan is being used to just boil water, my recipes specify *heavy* saucepans and skillets. My favorite saucepans are made by All-Clad. I prefer their practical Master Chef pans, which have a stainless steel interior for easy cleanup and a thick aluminum core for even heat. Some recipes specify a "nonreactive" pot or pan. This is usually called for when cooking a large amount of salt or acids. In an iron or copper pot, these ingredients can react and give foods an "off" or slightly metallic flavor.

Important measurements:
- A small saucepan has a 1- to 1½-quart capacity.
- A medium saucepan holds about 2 quarts.
- A large saucepan holds about 3 quarts.
- A pot holds 4 quarts, at minimum.

A stockpot does not need to be heavy. Look for an inexpensive aluminum one at a restaurant supply store.

Skillets and Sauté Pans

Look for a heavy-gauge skillet with a stainless interior for sautéing. The stainless steel won't react to acidic liquids and the heavy construction will ensure even cooking. Here, too, All-Clad is a good choice.

I like old-fashioned cast-iron skillets for frying because they cook evenly and caramelize foods well. Cast-iron skillets need TLC and they take a while to season. Look for used but well-maintained cast-iron skillets at thrift stores and yard sales.

Nonstick skillets are great when you're making an omelet or when you're trying to cut down on butter or oil, but some have concerns about their safety. If you do use a nonstick skillet, don't heat the pan while it is empty or put it in a hot oven, and be very careful to avoid scratching or chipping the surface.
- A small skillet measures about 5 to 6 inches across the bottom.
- A medium skillet is about 8 to 9 inches.
- A large skillet is 10 to 12 inches.
- A very large skillet measures more than 12 inches across the bottom and has tall sides, about 3 inches.

Dutch Ovens, French Ovens, Casseroles, and Braisers

Whatever you call them, cast-iron enameled pots with lids are a must. Stews, braises, fricassees, and pot roasts all taste better when cooked in these heavy, covered pots. Although they can be pricey, you get what you pay for with years of happy cooking. Staub is a high-quality brand with little "basting spikes" on the underside of the lid; Le Creuset and Lodge brands are excellent too. To economize, look for these pots at outlet stores.

Griddles

My stovetop is equipped with a griddle, and although I don't use it that often, it's great when I do. Grilled cheese sandwiches, quesadillas, pancakes, and French toast cook beautifully on the

well-seasoned, evenly heated, superflat surface. If you don't have one of these, griddle pans that fit over one or two burners and electric griddles are available. Because griddles are perfectly flat, they brown more evenly than skillets do, which are often subtly concave.

• • •

UTENSILS

Garlic Press

Chefs tend to be snobby about garlic presses—they don't like the pulverized result—but I love the strong flavor that the mashed bits lend to food. They're also great when you're in a hurry. Look for a self-cleaning garlic press so the holes don't get plugged with dried garlic.

Graters

Large-holed graters, or box graters, are perfect for cheese or vegetables, while small-holed graters are best for a fine shred of hard cheeses, such as Parmesan. Microplane® or other extra-sharp graters are perfect for grating citrus zest.

Juicers

If you have a citrus tree in your yard, or if you just love citrus, you should definitely own an electric juicer. Powered juicers are fast and efficient when a large amount of juice is called for, or if you want to freeze juice from your bumper crop for use later in the year.

Colorful Mexican press-style squeezers are also great. The orange (large), yellow (medium), and green (small) enameled aluminum juicers by Metaltex or Amco are useful when the juice of just one or two oranges or lemons is needed or when juicing key

or Mexican limes. The small, firm limes tend to slip from your fingers when using a standard juicer, but the little green squeezer works really quickly.

Two-chambered reamer juicers that strain and catch the juice in the jar/chamber below are an excellent low-cost option.

Ladles

Own a large one for soups and stews and a small one for batters and sauces.

Measuring Cups

Use measuring scoops for measuring dry ingredients and thick ingredients that need packing, such as peanut butter. The standard 1, ½, ⅓, and ¼ cup scoops are great, but measuring cup sets that also include ⅔ and ¾ cup scoops make measuring fast. I recommend having at least two sets, as stopping to wash dirty measuring cups while cooking can interrupt your flow.

Plastic and glass measuring cups are also a necessity in the kitchen. I use these for measuring liquids. Glass pitcher-style measuring cups are good for measuring hot liquids when making a reduction. Your kitchen should include a range from 1 cup to 8 cup measuring cups.

Measuring Spoons

Make sure that your measuring spoons are not too shallow—it's too difficult to measure accurately in them. I like having multiple sets so that I don't have to wash and dry between measuring.

Meat Tenderizer or Mallet

I have an aluminum mallet that I purchased at a restaurant supply store. It is large, with one smooth side and one textured side for tenderizing. It was very inexpensive and is perfect for flattening turkey and chicken breasts, and cracking nuts and whole spices.

Mixing Bowls and Multi-Purpose Bowls

Nesting metal bowls in various sizes are great for mixing and holding ingredients. Metal bowls are good for making a make-shift double boiler. Egg whites should always be beaten in metal bowls as the whites stick better to the sides, resulting in airy meringues. Ceramic bowls can be used for mixing and serving. Large earthenware bowls can be used for salad and for raising bread dough. An assortment of little bowls is handy for setting up your *mise en place*.

Mortar and Pestle

I have a few mortars and pestles—some I use and some I don't. The Mexican *molcajete*, made out of volcanic rock, doesn't get out much, but the small, grooved porcelain bowl with a wooden pestle lives on the kitchen counter. The rough interior of the bowl makes quick work of grinding small spices.

Parchment Paper

Parchment paper is great for lining pans when baking.

Pastry Brushes

I prefer the simple wooden ones with natural fibers.

Rolling Pins

I use my grandmother's "rolling" rolling pin with handles when I make pie dough; it feels right. I use a French-style (nonrolling) pin made of copper when working with large amounts of dough or pastry. I have used silicone rolling pins, fancy heavyweight models, and inexpensive nonstick rolling pins, and they all work beautifully. The key is to find a rolling pin that feels comfortable to you.

Salad Spinner

A salad spinner is a must, especially for those who grow their own lettuce. Moisture is what leads to decay on the delicate leaves, so it's very important to dry your greens. I wash, dry, and store my greens in my salad spinner.

Silicone Pan Liners

Silicone liners, such as the ones made by Silpat®, are expensive, but they can be used over and over again (saving paper and trees). Silicone provides an excellent nonstick baking surface, a safeguard against burned cookies, and it does not need to be greased.

Skewers and Toothpicks

Bamboo skewers are great for making kebabs and for testing doneness in baked goods. Decorative metal skewers look cool and don't burn on the grill. Toothpicks are good for securing stuffed or wrapped foods.

Spatulas: Metal and Silicone

Spatulas are used for turning and flipping. Offset and narrow spatulas work best for frosting cakes and leveling batters. Silicone spatulas are best for stirring custards and fruit-based mixtures on the stovetop, and for scraping batter out of mixing bowls.

Slotted Spoons

Slotted spoons are used to remove solids from liquid. They come in all sizes and shapes—I like the large spoons with a few slots.

Strainers and Colanders

Equip your kitchen with a large colander with large holes for draining pasta and for washing vegetables, a medium strainer with medium mesh for straining and sifting, and a smaller, fine-meshed strainer for removing seeds from juices or small solids from liquids.

Thermometers

An instant-read thermometer is a must. I use my thermometer

whenever I cook meat or poultry. With meat, the temperature tells me exactly when it's cooked to a perfect medium-rare, and when cooking poultry, the gauge tells me when it is safe to eat. A candy or deep-fry thermometer is good for determining egg safety in custards, deep frying, and candy making.

Tongs

I buy tongs at restaurant supply stores. I like the lightweight, cheaper ones as they are easy to pinch. More expensive, heavier gauge tongs fatigue my hands. I have three pairs: small and medium for the kitchen and long ones for the barbecue.

Twine or Silicone Food Loops

Essential for tying roasts and trussing, spools of kitchen string are available at some markets, hardware and kitchen stores. Silicone trussing tools, such as the Food Loop, are convenient as they have easy-to-use closing clips (so you don't have to fumble with knots) and are heat-proof, non-stick, and reusable.

Vegetable Peeler

My favorite peeler is by OXO; it feels good in my hand and the blade has stayed sharp for well over 10 years. There are many fancy peelers at cookware stores today—some with slightly serrated edges that can peel tomatoes. But, really, how often does one need to peel a tomato?

Whisks

Buy three for essential whisking tasks: a small one for vinaigrette, a medium one for batters, and a large one for whipping cream or egg whites.

Wooden Spoons

Wooden spoons are old-fashioned favorites of mine. I like them for sautéing, especially onions. They are easy going with no unpleasant metal-against-metal scraping as you stir and sauté. But don't use wooden spoons that have stirred onions and garlic on fruit or custards, as the wood can impart an unpleasant flavor.

Simple Kitchen Garden Guide

When you throw yourself into gardening as a novice, the successes, like a pleasant surprise, overshadow the failures. We certainly don't grow all of our own fruits and vegetables, but gardening has allowed our family to connect with nature and play a healthy part in the food chain. Here is a simple overview of how to start an edible garden. For more information, check out books specific to your growing zone.

Each part of the country falls into an agricultural zone on the USDA's "plant hardiness zone-map." The zones provide a planting guideline geared to each specific climate. You can find your zone by going to the USDA website at www.usda.gov. The zones can be confusing, as the USDA zones often conflict with a regional system of climate zones. For instance, I live in zone 9 according to the USDA and zone 20 in the West. To ensure planting success, consult with your local independent nursery. These folks have the knowledge and experience necessary for planting in your locale or microclimate. Another good resource is your local cooperative extension service. Through a national website—www.csrees.usda.gov/Extension— you can get in touch with master gardeners, fruit tree specialists, and other experts who understand your local climate and growing conditions best.

• • •

LOCATION

Find a flat place in your yard that gets about 6 hours of full sunlight a day. If you don't have a yard, many plants grow well in pots and containers on a sunny patio, roof, or terrace. If you don't have a place to plant a garden at home, consider becoming part of a community garden. In my neighborhood, the Eaglerockdale Community Garden provides us a place to grow what we don't have room to grow at home. It's a wonderful place to meet and learn from other gardeners. To find a community garden in your neighborhood, talk to your local city council's office.

• • •

BED PREPARATION

In the landscape trade, bed preparation can make or break an installation. In vegetable gardening, bed preparation should be taken very seriously. Vegetables grow best when cultivated in raised beds. The raised bed (often made from 2 by 12-inch pieces of lumber set up as, say, a 5 by 10-foot rectangle) gives the soil a lift to begin with, as it is contained on all four sides, and then consolidates the soil's ingredients, to concentrate them on the vegetables.

It helps to have good dirt (soil) in your yard to begin with, but whatever soil you have, it will need amending. Fill your raised bed about halfway with dirt (the dirt in and around where the bed is installed is fine). Then add enough compost—either your own, from a bulk carrier, or from bags bought at a retail nursery—fill the raised bed, leaving a couple of inches at the top. If you buy compost from the nursery, use the organic kind that contains trace amounts of natural fertilizers. Test the soil if you are unsure about the quality. A test-kit is available at garden centers. The ideal pH of soil is 7.

If your soil tests higher, decrease the acidity by adding lime, and if it is too low, add more compost.

Next, perform some double digging, which involves mixing the soil that is originally from your garden with compost. This is important because it makes it easy for the roots of your vegetables to grow, and a good root system makes for robust and healthy plants. Using a shovel, dig as deep as you can, then turn the soil, mixing it thoroughly. Add some organic fertilizer, like Gro Power Plus 5-3-1 or Bio-Start, while lifting and turning the soil (following the directions on the fertilizer package). Repeat this process to loosen the soil even further.

. . .

COMPOST

Good compost is essential to successful vegetable gardening. Composting is nature's way of creating topsoil through the decomposition of organic matter. Start a compost pile in your yard or community garden. We use a composting bin that was provided by our city's refuse department to encourage composting and lessen the amount of trash hauling. Composting bins are available at home and garden supply stores or online.

Composting begins in your kitchen. Keep a small pail next to the sink, and add vegetable peels, coffee grounds, eggshells, and other plant-based material. Transfer the pail to the compost pile as it fills. Avoid putting any protein into the compost, as you don't want to attract critters.

Our compost routine has worked its way into part of our everyday household life. Okay . . . it's become one of the chores. But chores aren't *all* bad. This one can be as rewarding as concocting a brilliant cup of coffee. The morning visit to our compost coincides with the feeding of the chickens and goat, and therein lies one of nature's perfect pairings. Twice a week, the compost is supplemented—not just by the usual kitchen scraps, old cut flowers, and garden clippings—but also by a solid shot of goat and chicken manure. This gets topped off by 3 to 4 inches of oak leaves and, bingo, a perfect recipe. This mixture "cooks" for a month, then we've got coveted fertilizer and are the talk of the community garden.

One thing to keep in mind when working with compost is the carbon/nitrogen ratio. Simply put, you need the right ratio of "brown things" (carbon)—hedge clippings, tomato vines, leaves, and straw—to "green things" (nitrogen)—fresh grass clippings, chicken manure, green weeds, and old bedding plants. The ideal ratio is 30:1 carbon to nitrogen. All plants and manure contain both carbon and nitrogen. A simple rule of thumb is that if your compost is dry, it has too much carbon and if it is wet and gushy, it has too much nitrogen.

Mixing the compost is very important. Use a pointed shovel or pitchfork to turn all of the composted materials regularly. As you add to and work with the contents in your bin, after a few weeks the matter at the bottom of the pile will be good and ready to add to your garden's topsoil.

CONVERSION TABLES

Formulas for Metric Conversion

Ounces to grams	multiply ounces by 28.35
Pounds to grams	multiply pounds by 453.5
Cups to liters	multiply cups by .24
Fahrenheit to Centigrade	subtract 32 from Fahrenheit, multiply by five and divide by 9

Metric Equivalents for Volume

U.S.		Metric
⅛ tsp.		0.6 ml
½ tsp.		2.5 ml
¾ tsp.		4.0 ml
1 tsp.		5.0 ml
1½ tsp.		7.0 ml
2 tsp.		10.0 ml
3 tsp.		15.0 ml
4 tsp.		20.0 ml
1 Tbsp.	—	15.0 ml
1½ Tbsp.	—	22.0 ml
2 Tbsp. (⅛ cup)	1 fl. oz	30.0 ml
2½ Tbsp.	—	37.0 ml
3 Tbsp.	—	44.0 ml
⅓ cup	—	57.0 ml
4 Tbsp. (¼ cup)	2 fl. oz	59.0 ml
5 Tbsp.	—	74.0 ml
6 Tbsp.	—	89.0 ml
8 Tbsp. (½ cup)	4 fl. oz	120.0 ml
¾ cup	6 fl. oz	178.0 ml
1 cup	8 fl. oz	237.0 ml (.24 liters)
1½ cups	—	354.0 ml
1¾ cups	—	414.0 ml
2 cups (1 pint)	16 fl. oz	473.0 ml
4 cups (1 quart)	32 fl. oz	(.95 liters)
5 cups	—	(1.183 liters)
16 cups (1 gallon)	128 fl. oz	(3.8 liters)

Oven Temperatures

Degrees Fahrenheit	Degrees Centigrade	British Gas Marks
200°	93°	—
250°	120°	—
275°	140°	1
300°	150°	2
325°	165°	3
350°	175°	4
375°	190°	5
400°	200°	6
450°	230°	8

Metric Equivalents for Weight

U.S.	Metric
1 oz	28 g
2 oz	58 g
3 oz	85 g
4 oz (¼ lb.)	113 g
5 oz	142 g
6 oz	170 g
7 oz	199 g
8 oz (½ lb.)	227 g
10 oz	284 g
12 oz (¾ lb.)	340 g
14 oz	397 g
16 oz (1 lb.)	454 g

Metric Equivalents for Butter

U.S.	Metric
2 tsp.	10.0 g
1 Tbsp.	15.0 g
1½ Tbsp.	22.5 g
2 Tbsp. (1 oz)	55.0 g
3 Tbsp.	70.0 g
¼ lb. (1 stick)	110.0 g
½ lb. (2 sticks)	220.0 g

Metric Equivalents for Length

U.S.	Metric
¼ inch	.65 cm
½ inch	1.25 cm
1 inch	2.50 cm
2 inches	5.00 cm
3 inches	6.00 cm
4 inches	8.00 cm
5 inches	11.00 cm
6 inches	15.00 cm
7 inches	18.00 cm
8 inches	20.00 cm
9 inches	23.00 cm
12 inches	30.50 cm
15 inches	38.00 cm

PEST CONTROL

Although the species of common garden pests may vary from region to region, methods of combating insects are the same for all gardens. Pests such as earwigs and pill bugs can munch their way through tender seedlings at such a speed that an entire crop of newly germinated plants can be obliterated overnight. It may sound simplistic, but one way of controlling pests is to maintain a tidy garden. Insects do most of their damage at night, and in the day they retreat to moist, dark, hidden places like piles of rubbish and stacks of junk. Removing the daytime habitat of choice for the pests really helps subdue them, and it also helps beautify your yard.

Growing a variety of plants together, known as *companion planting*, also keeps bugs at bay. An example of companion planting is the mixing of beans or peas with corn. The vines fix atmospheric nitrogen, meaning that the peas or beans transfer nitrogen from the air to the soil and the corn, a heavy nitrogen feeder, benefits. In our vegetable beds we plant lots of marigolds, which are supposed to

inhibit detrimental nematodes (microscopic worms). Among the tomatoes we poke basil, which is purported to inhibit insects and diseases that plague tomatoes. You can also grow certain plants that attract beneficial insects. Lady bugs—so famous for eating aphids—are attracted to yarrow, feverfew, cosmos, or sweet alyssum. These plants can be planted from seed or from small plants purchased at the nursery around your vegetable planting areas.

We prefer not to use pesticides in our garden, but if bugs are a persistent problem in your yard, consider using a natural pesticide such as an insecticidal soap or *Bacillus thuringiensis* (known as Bt), a plant-derived bacterium used for pest control. You can get these products and information regarding their use at your local nursery.

GROWING VEGETABLES

Planting Seasons

Spring is the main planting season for vegetables in all zones. A spring planting yields a summer harvest. You can begin your garden after the last frost by sowing seeds or transplanting starts. Starts are small plants that are purchased from the nursery (often in six-packs) or grown from seed in small pots indoors or in a greenhouse. For us, planting for our summer beds might include tomatoes, basil, melons, and (we stress) tomatoes. Other good vegetables to plant in the spring are cucumbers, beans, corn, peppers, eggplant, okra, and squash.

Spring and Fall Plantings

You can also grow certain vegetables in the early spring. In zones as far north as zone 5, radishes, turnips, and green onions can be sown for harvest after only about a month or two of growing time, allowing the vegetable bed to be planted again for a summer harvest.

In fall, vegetables such as carrots, beets, broccoli, cabbage, cauliflower, Brussels sprouts, onions, and radishes can be planted to reach maturity before the first freezing temperatures in colder climes. In warmer zones, Swiss chard, spinach, and peas can be added to the list.

Seeds and plants perform differently in various climates, so again, I stress how important it is to consult local experts before planting your vegetable garden.

Tomatoes

Like a freshly laid egg, homegrown tomatoes hold no comparison to tomatoes from the supermarket or even the farmers' market. Except for cherry tomatoes and canned tomatoes, I avoid tomatoes when they are not in season. During summer and into early fall, we gorge on tomatoes, enjoying thick slices on buttered or olive oil–drizzled toast for lunch, and our dinners always feature sliced tomatoes sprinkled with sea salt and herbs. By the time we've eaten the last thick-skinned, green-shouldered fruit off the withering vine, we are so sated, there is almost a bit of relief in the knowledge that we will not see another till summer.

Tomato cultivation and care is fairly universal. We begin our tomato garden with plants purchased at the nursery. Plant starts in the ground after any danger of frost is passed. Tomatoes need full sun and rich, well-draining, cultivated soil. They are one of the few plants that are planted deep in the soil (3- to 4-inches). Water tomatoes carefully and deeply; avoid watering the foliage. Do not let tomatoes dry out between watering, as inconsistent moisture can cause blossom rot, a condition that results in a dead, brown area at

the base, or blossom end, of the tomato. Tomatoes are heavy feeders, so make sure your soil is properly amended. Thorough cultivation—"double digging"—can stave off diseases. Keep smokers away from your tomatoes, as diseases from tobacco are transmitted easily to the plants through handling—and a tobacco-related disease can wipe out an entire tomato planting.

Many arboretums, public gardens, and nurseries hold "Tomato-mania"-type events, where you can gather knowledge and supplies from tomato experts and enthusiasts. We grow an assortment of tomatoes: tiny and large, yellow, orange, pink and red, heirloom, and hybrids. I like the flavor and uniqueness of the heirloom tomatoes, but I also like the high yield, uniform size, shape, and disease-resistance of hybrids such a Better Boy and Lemon Boy. We make our own tomato cages out of wire mesh made for reinforcing concrete (available at building supply stores). We like the sturdy cages with large holes that allow us to reach into the cages and pick the fruit. Prefabricated tomato cages are available at nurseries, and garden stakes can also be used to prop up tomato vines.

Green Garlic

Green garlic is to garlic what green onions are to the onion. It is fun to grow, and you can start it from a garlic bulb purchased at the market. Plant the garlic in the early spring. Separate the bulb into individual cloves, but don't peel them. Plant the cloves in rows four inches apart, about 1 to 2 inches deep, root side down (pointed side up), and cover them with soil. Keep the soil moist but not soggy. Enjoy the young bulbs and greens. Unharvested green garlic will mature into garlic bulbs.

Salad Greens

I can't say enough about the benefits of growing your own lettuce. Bags of washed salad greens are a wonderful convenience, but the flavor of freshly picked greens is so extraordinary that it is definitely

worth the effort if you have the time and space to grow them.

All lettuces should be grown in loose soil with good drainage. In warmer zones (8 and 9) like mine, lettuce can be grown with successive plantings in the fall, winter, and spring in the full sun. In the summer, we grow lettuce in partial shade or under a protective shade cloth. In cooler climates (zones 4 to 7), grow lettuce in the summer growing season in full sun. An easy, hassle-free though not particularly cost-effective way to grow lettuce is from "starts"—small individual plants, usually sold in six-packs at nurseries.

Loose-leaf and romaine lettuces are easy to grow from seeds or starts. Loose-leaf lettuces form rosettes as they grow, take a good amount of sun without bolting (blooming and going to seed) too quickly, and come in several varieties from red and green oak leaf to green ice and salad bowl. Romaine lettuce grows into large, tall heads and come in several varieties—"Freckles" is an interesting red-speckled Romaine.

Growing lettuce from a seed packet of Mesclun mix is another excellent option. Mesclun mixes are a good choice for growing greens as they contain hearty, fast-growing varieties of lettuce, mustards, arugula, cress, chicory, and mizuna. The last batch of seeds we planted surprised us with delicate chervil fronds. Another advantage of growing mesclun is that you thin by harvesting the baby plants for a delicate salad while allowing the other plants to mature into larger heads.

· · ·

HERBS

Herbs—such as oregano, marjoram, sage, rosemary, and thyme—are hearty perennials, which means they do not need to be replanted each season and they often live for more than two years. In mild climates, you can use these herbs to punctuate your plantings.

In our garden, herbs mingle with succulents, shrubs, and flowers in planters. In cooler climates (zones 6 to 8), perennial herbs need extra care to make it through the winter. A fall pruning and a light, loose mulching should do the job. If the weather gets really cold (zones 4 and 5), the plants should be potted and placed indoors for winter. All of these herbs require several hours of direct sunlight each

day, good-draining soil, and consistent watering that keeps the roots neither too wet nor too dry.

Mint, tarragon, and chives are perennials that die back completely or go dormant in the winter. Mint grows like a weed in our garden. It even pops up among our potted orchids. It loves water; we grow it around the hose faucets at the community garden. Mint all but vanishes in the winter, but come spring and summer, there is plenty to flavor teas, salads, and cocktails. Tarragon also pops up each spring, at the same time as the dahlias return. Outside of high altitudes and cold climates, tarragon will grow just about anywhere. Also pleasantly surprising are the delicate green shoots sent up each spring by a tuft of chives planted 10 years ago. Chives are from the onion family, and the bulbs can be planted in a pot and kept on a windowsill. Chives have the added bonus of blooming pretty purple-pink flowers.

Basil and parsley are annuals. Annuals are plants that live only one growing season and need to be replanted each year. Like summer vegetables, basil and parsley are grown from spring into summer. Basil is very easy to grow and does well in pots—you just have to protect the tender young plants from hungry bugs. Plant enough basil, at least a six-pack of starts, to make a batch of pesto. I love flat-leaf Italian parsley (the curly-leafed variety is French parsley). A little bit adds a fresh flavor and color to just about any dish. I also grow parsley from nursery starts.

Two culinary shrubs that we love are lemon verbena (Latin name *Aloysia Triphylla*) and sweet bay or Turkish laurel (Latin name *Laurus Nobilus*). Lemon verbena is a deciduous or semi-evergreen shrub native to Argentina and Chile. Called *la verveine* in France, is popular in Provence, where the lemon-scented leaves are used to flavor teas and perfume soaps. The herb can grow into a large, gangling shrub, about 6 feet tall. Throughout Spain, you'll see sweet bay pruned into topiaries in terracotta pots at building entrances. The dark, green-leafed Mediterranean shrub, which can grow into a tree, is easy to grow. It's not fussy about soil, but it needs good drainage. We have a row of the tall shrubs planted as a privacy screen. The fragrant leaves find their way into our soups and stews and are a nice addition to floral arrangements. Verbena and sweet bay are hearty and can flourish carefree in zones 8 to 10. In zones 5 to 7, plant the shrubs in pots and bring them indoors for the winter.

• • •

FRUIT TREES

Deciduous fruit trees are a lovely way to complete your garden. They change with the seasons—the branches are full of blossoms in early spring, leafy and laden with fruit in the summer, brown and near naked in the fall, and bare in the winter. There's a perfect fruit tree for just about every zone. Gardeners up north can grow apples and pears. Further south you might try sour cherries, plums, and apricots, and in the Midwest you can add nectarines and peaches to the list. Your local nurseries will carry appropriate species and varieties for your garden, and they can give you advice as to how and where to plant them.

In our garden, we have a plum and an apricot tree. Before we began construction on our house, we found a good place to plant a Santa Rosa plum tree because for me, a Santa Rosa is the taste of summer. My grandmother had a giant, knobby-gnarly Santa Rosa in her backyard, and every summery my sister and I would feast on the plums. My Nana also made the most amazing stewed plums from the deep red-fleshed fruit. The Santa Rosa plum is self-pollinating, which means you only need to plant one tree. There is a plum tree appropriate for just about every climate.

Our apricot tree is called "Gold Kissed." I love the small, super flavorful apricots from this tree and am looking forward to the day

when it is so abundant that the neighborhood squirrels can't eat all the fruit and will leave some for me. It's important to note that apricot trees fruit on second-year growth (meaning that the branches sprouting after pruning will not flower until the following year), so it is best to prune judiciously and to leave enough old growth in order to have fruit year after year.

• • •

Growing citrus trees is limited to zones 9 and 10 in the USDA hardiness zones. This is because high heat is required to produce sweet citrus fruit. Grapefruit, oranges, and tangerines grow best in California, Texas, Arizona, and Florida. Some of my favorites are the Bearss lime, the Moro blood orange, the Meyer lemon, and the Kaffir Lime tree.

• • •

Bearss Lime Trees
The seedless, juicy Bearss or Persian limes are pale green and almost yellow when fully ripened. The main fruit crop is in winter or late spring, but there are usually a few limes on the tree year-round.

Moro Blood Orange Trees

I first ate a blood orange in France when I was 16 years old. I was in complete wonder of this juicy, dark raspberry–hued and flavored orange. The Moro can tolerate less heat than navel or Valencia oranges, and can still produce good fruit. It keeps an attractive shape with minimal pruning.

Meyer Lemon Trees

Meyer lemon trees, sometimes labeled "improved Meyer," produce rounder, thinner-skinned, and less acidic than the standard Eureka lemon tree. The Meyer bears fruit year-round and begins to yield fruit at a young age, so they're the perfect to plant anytime. Smaller than other lemon varieties, the plant can grow in a large pot. The Meyer lemon is such a forgiving plant that it is a good candidate to grow in non-citrus growing zones. Planted in a container, the Meyer could bask in the sun in the summer, and when the threat of frost nears, the small tree can be moved to a greenhouse or solarium to ride out the winter.

Kaffir Lime Trees

The small pretty tree with aromatic figure-eight-shaped double leaves is easy to grow and care for. The tree, prized in Southeast Asia, grows well in a pot, and like all citrus, needs lots of sun. Because the tree is so small (often the size of a small houseplant) and because it's grown primarily for it's flavorful leaves and not its acrid, wrinkled fruit, folks who live in colder climates should consider nurturing this exotic potted tree. Let it soak up the sun outdoors in summer and bring it indoors for the winter.

How to Follow a Recipe

This may seem like a no-brainer, but it's worth saying nonetheless. The first thing you need to do when cooking with a recipe is to read the recipe *all the way through* before you begin to check for any long marinating, chilling, soaking, or cooking times. This is important to make sure you have enough time to make the dish. It also helps you determine if you have all the ingredients you need.

Ingredients are listed in the order that they are used in a recipe. A space between the list of ingredients indicates a new step or process, or a break in time.

Mise en Place—This is a French term we learn in culinary school, and it literally means "setting in place." In the kitchen, it refers to having all your ingredients prepared and ready to go into the recipe. So, *before* you start cooking, look at the list of ingredients required, and peel, core, slice, dice, chop, or mince whatever necessary. You don't have to go so far as to have liquids measured; just have a measuring cup at the ready.

APPETIZERS
AND SMALL PLATES

Burrata Cheese with Fresh Pesto Drizzle

Burrata cheese is the Rolls Royce of fresh mozzarella. The soft, creamy cheese is basically mozzarella stuffed with mozzarella curd and heavy cream. It has an unbelievable milky-sweet flavor. If it's too hard to find, just drizzle the pesto over goat cheese to mimic Burrata's spreadable softness.

YIELD: 8 SERVINGS

Pesto

2 cups basil leaves, lightly packed

½ cup pine nuts, toasted

½ cup grated Parmigiano-Reggiano cheese

3 garlic cloves

¼ cup extra-virgin olive oil

Salt

Assembly

¼ cup extra-virgin olive oil

Sea salt

16 ounces Burrata cheese

1 cup yellow and red grape
  or cherry tomatoes, cut in half

Basil sprigs

Baguette, sliced

To make the pesto: Combine the basil, pine nuts, Parmigiano-Reggiano, and garlic in the bowl of a food processor. Pulse until the mixture is finely chopped. Add the olive oil and roughly purée. Season the pesto with salt. *(Can be prepared up to 4 days ahead. Transfer the pesto to a small container and cover with plastic wrap, pressed directly onto the pesto; refrigerate.)*

To assemble the dish: Combine ½ cup of the pesto with the olive oil in a small bowl. Thin with 2 to 4 tablespoons water, 1 tablespoon at a time. Season with salt.

Drain the Burrata, if necessary, and place in a dish. Gently break open the cheese and drizzle it with the pesto mixture. Surround it decoratively with tomatoes. Sprinkle with sea salt, garnish with basil sprigs, and serve with sliced baguette.

Other ideas: You can also use this pesto on pasta, diluted with a bit of heavy cream, or spread it on toast and top with a fried egg, sliced tomato, and Parmesan cheese.

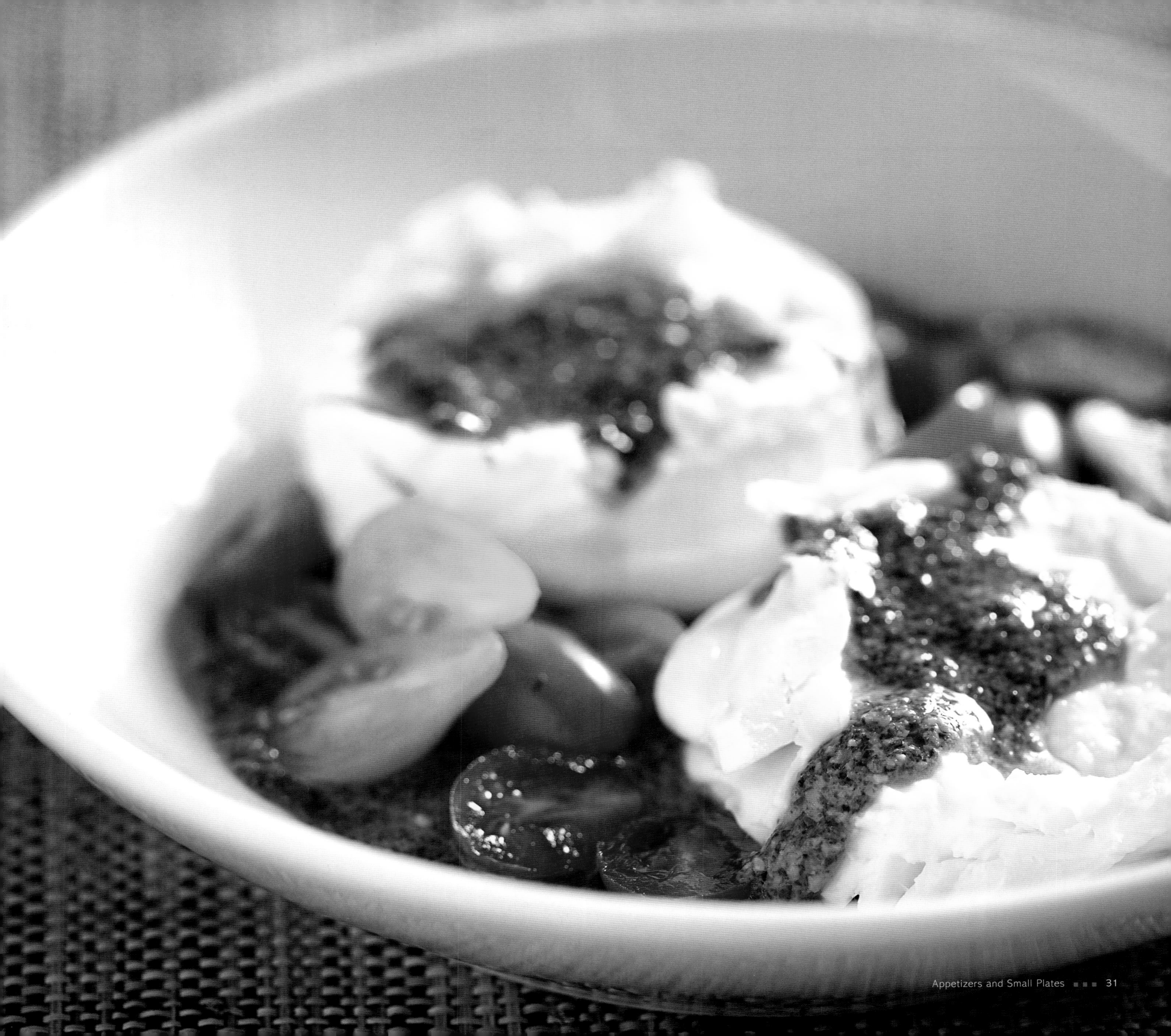

Mango Spring Rolls with Peanut Sauce

I like to bring these Vietnamese-inspired spring rolls to those parties where you are asked to bring an appetizer. Because they are not fried, they are relatively easy to make, and are really impressive. I also make these for a light lunch or as a prelude to the Beef Pho on page 54.

YIELD: 12 SPRING ROLLS

Peanut Sauce
½ cup natural-style creamy peanut butter
2 tablespoons light brown sugar,
   firmly packed
1 tablespoon nam pla (Thai fish sauce)
1 teaspoon Thai red curry paste

Spring Rolls
½ English hothouse cucumber
12 (6-inch) rice paper rounds
12 very large basil leaves
¾ cup mint leaves, lightly packed
24 cilantro sprigs
1 slightly firm mango, thinly sliced

To make the sauce: Whisk together the peanut butter, brown sugar, nam pla, curry paste, and ½ cup water in a medium-sized bowl. (*The sauce can be prepared up to 2 days ahead. Cover and refrigerate.*)

To make the spring rolls: Cut the cucumber into matchsticks about 2½-inches long and ¼-inch thick. Fill a large bowl with warm water. Working in batches, soak three of the rice paper rounds in the water until softened, about 2 minutes. Remove the rounds from the water and arrange in a single layer on a work surface.

Place 1 basil leaf in the center of a round and sprinkle with 1 tablespoon of the mint leaves. Place 2 cilantro sprigs atop the mint. Place 2 mango strips, then 2 cucumber strips atop the cilantro. Fold one edge of the round over the filling. Fold in the ends and roll up the rice paper round tightly, enclosing the filling. Transfer to a platter. Repeat with the remaining rice paper rounds and fillings.

Cover the rolls with moist paper towels, then plastic wrap and chill. (*The rolls can be prepared up to 6 hours ahead. Keep chilled.*)

To serve, slice the rolls in half and serve with the peanut sauce.

Interesting Thai Ingredients

Nam pla, or Thai fish sauce, is made from fermented anchovies. It sounds gross, and the smell is akin to a fish emulsion for the garden, but Thai food simply wouldn't taste right without it. Straight, it tastes like salty, fishy sea water, but in soups, stews, and sauces, nam pla adds a deep, salty flavor that soy sauce can't match. Store nam pla at cool room temperature.

Thai curry pastes come in red, green, and yellow varieties. All three contain chile, garlic, lemongrass, and galangal. The green variety features green chiles, the red features red chiles, and the yellow features turmeric. All are very spicy—a little goes a long way. In this recipe, I call for red curry paste, as it is the most readily available, but any variety can be used. Two teaspoons of the paste mixed with 1 tablespoon fresh lime juice and 1 tablespoon vegetable oil makes a delicious marinade for four 6-ounce salmon fillets.

Nam pla and Thai curry paste are available at specialty foods stores and Thai markets.

Herbed Crab Cakes with Salad and Lemon-Herb Vinaigrette

Most restaurant and ready-made crab cakes are a bready disappointment. These have just a few Japanese bread crumbs, called panko, and an interesting combination of fresh herbs. The combination of dill, tarragon, and cilantro gives these delicate crab cakes a bright, fresh, herb flavor. If you prefer, you can streamline the recipe by using only 2 tablespoons of dill or tarragon instead of the trio below. I like crab cakes with a bit of salad, but you could leave that out, too.

YIELD: 8 CRAB CAKES, 4 SERVINGS

Crab Cakes

1 green onion, minced

2 tablespoons mayonnaise,
   preferably organic

1 egg yolk

1 tablespoon fresh lemon juice

2 teaspoons minced fresh dill

2 teaspoons minced fresh tarragon

2 teaspoons minced fresh cilantro

1 teaspoon Dijon mustard

1 teaspoon grated lemon zest

8 ounces blue or Dungeness crabmeat

1½ cups panko

Salt and pepper

2 tablespoons unsalted butter

1 tablespoon grapeseed oil

Salad

¼ cup grapeseed oil

2 tablespoons fresh lemon juice

2 teaspoons minced fresh dill

2 teaspoons minced fresh tarragon

2 teaspoons minced fresh cilantro

2 teaspoons minced green onion

¼ teaspoon Dijon mustard

Salt and pepper

4 cups baby lettuces (such as arugula,
   mizuna, mâche, and frisée), lightly packed

To make the crab cakes: Whisk the green onion, mayonnaise, egg yolk, lemon juice, dill, tarragon, cilantro, mustard, and lemon zest in a large bowl. Gently mix in the crab meat and ½ cup of the panko. Season the mixture with salt and pepper and let it stand for 10 minutes.

Line a baking sheet with waxed paper. Sprinkle the remaining 1 cup panko onto another baking sheet.

Form the crab mixture into eight 2-inch patties, using a scant ¼ cup for each. Press both sides of the patties gently into the panko to coat both sides lightly and evenly. Transfer the crab cakes to the other baking sheet. Cover with plastic wrap and refrigerate for 1 hour or up to overnight.

To make the salad: Whisk the grapeseed oil, lemon juice, dill, tarragon, cilantro, green onion, and mustard in a small bowl. Season the vinaigrette to taste with salt and pepper. Toss the salad with just enough vinaigrette to lightly coat the greens.

To cook the crab cakes: Heat the butter and grapeseed oil in a heavy, large nonstick skillet set over medium to medium-high heat. Add the crab cakes and cook, 2 to 3 minutes per side, until golden brown on each side.

Place the crab cakes on plates and surround them with a small amount of salad. Drizzle the crab cakes with a little vinaigrette and serve.

Roasted Dates
with Applewood-Smoked Bacon

A Deglet Noor date is a firm date—you can often find them pitted. While a softer date, such as a Medjool, can be substituted in this recipe, they tend to be a little sticky to work with and a bit gooey to eat. Here, the dates are roasted, bringing out their concentrated salty, sweet, smoky, rich flavors. They are satisfying without being filling. Double or triple the recipe as necessary. I make this in my toaster oven, which I love. I can roast, toast, and broil without using the energy and time required to heat my conventional oven. It makes this dish a snap to make on the spur of the moment and one of my favorite things to serve friends before dinner.

YIELD: ABOUT 2 SERVINGS

2 slices applewood-smoked bacon
6 Deglet Noor Dates, pitted

Preheat the toaster oven to 400°F. Line the toaster oven pan with aluminum foil.

Cut each bacon slice into 3 even pieces. Wrap a piece around each date and secure with a toothpick. Arrange the dates on the prepared pan. Roast until the bacon is browned on all sides, turning once, about 12 minutes. Cool the dates slightly. Carefully remove the toothpick and serve warm on small plates.

Pancetta Crisps with Goat Cheese and Fuyu Persimmons

This treat is a version of an appetizer created by my good friend Sarah Tenaglia, senior food editor at *Bon Appétit* magazine. Sarah's canapé featured pears, but a basket of persimmons inspired my adaptation. Fuyu persimmons are small, tomato-shaped fruit that are firm when ripe, and non-astringent, setting them apart from the larger, acorn-shaped Hachiya variety. Both persimmon trees are native to China and grow well in a Mediterranean climate. Pancetta is Italian bacon that is cured with salt and spices but is not smoked. Here, salty, sweet, and creamy combine in an easy, elegant, autumn appetizer that's great with Champagne.

YIELD: 6 TO 8 SERVINGS

5 ounces soft goat cheese
1 teaspoon minced fresh thyme
2 small Fuyu persimmons
16 thin slices pancetta, about 3 ounces
Pepper
Fresh thyme leaves, for serving

Preheat the oven to 450°F.

Mix the goat cheese and thyme in a small bowl. Cut each persimmon into 8 small wedges.

Place the pancetta in a single layer on a large, rimmed baking sheet. Sprinkle with pepper. Bake the pancetta until it is golden brown and crisp, about 10 minutes.

Using a spatula, slide the pancetta crisps onto a platter. Top each crisp with about 1 slightly rounded teaspoon of the goat cheese mixture and 1 persimmon wedge. Sprinkle with thyme leaves and serve.

Hummus with Jalapeño-Cilantro Pesto

Hummus is a versatile Middle Eastern dip, and this one has a spicy pesto swirl, adding a touch of color and burst of flavor. It's a healthful snack when served with carrot sticks and crackers, a vegetarian option at cocktail parties, and an integral part of any Middle Eastern feast. My favorite way to serve this dip is on grilled flatbread topped with crumbled feta. Tahini is toasted sesame seed paste. It's available at Middle Eastern markets, health food stores, and some supermarkets.

YIELD: ABOUT 4 CUPS

Pesto

1 cup cilantro sprigs, packed

⅓ cup chopped flat-leaf parsley, packed

2 green onions, trimmed
   and cut into 1-inch pieces

1 to 2 jalapeño chiles, stems removed

⅓ cup extra-virgin olive oil

1 garlic clove

Salt and pepper

Hummus

2 (15-ounce) cans garbanzo beans,
   preferably organic

½ cup plus 2 tablespoons fresh lemon juice

½ cup tahini

⅓ cup extra-virgin olive oil

3 garlic cloves

Salt

Fresh pita bread

To make the pesto: Combine the cilantro, parsley, green onions, jalapeños, olive oil, and garlic in a food processor and blend until smooth. Using a rubber spatula, transfer the pesto to a small bowl; season with salt and pepper to taste. (Do not wash the processor bowl.)

To make the hummus: Drain the garbanzo beans, reserving ½ cup of the liquid. Combine the garbanzo beans, reserved liquid, lemon juice, tahini, olive oil, and garlic in the bowl of a food processor and process until smooth. Season with salt to taste. Transfer to a medium-sized bowl. *(The hummus and pesto can be prepared up to 4 days ahead. Cover separately and refrigerate.)*

To serve, make an indentation in the center of the hummus with a large spoon. Spoon the pesto into the indentation and swirl gently. Serve with pita bread.

Salty-Sweet-Spicy Almonds

Red pepper flakes, fennel seeds, a touch of sugar and salt make these nuts a great cocktail snack.

YIELD: 2 CUPS

⅓ cup sugar
1 tablespoon fennel seeds
2 teaspoons salt
2 teaspoons crushed red pepper flakes
2 cups raw almonds

Preheat the oven to 325°F. Line a heavy baking sheet with aluminum foil and spray with nonstick cooking spray.

Mix the sugar, fennel seeds, salt, and red pepper flakes in a medium-sized bowl. Add the almonds and 2 tablespoons water and stir until the nuts are well coated. Pour the nut mixture onto the foil and spread in one layer.

Bake the nuts until the sugar mixture melts, about 5 minutes. Stir. Continue baking and stirring until the nuts are deep golden brown and glazed, about 17 minutes longer.

Remove the almonds from the oven and separate the nuts slightly with a fork. Cool completely. Transfer the almonds to a bowl. (*The almonds can be prepared 4 days ahead and stored in ziptop bag.*)

Marinated Feta and Olives

I feature this dish at all of my big parties since I can make a double or triple batch and make it a week ahead—it is great as part of a buffet. I've been known to make a complete supper of this easy appetizer, with a handful of fresh-picked greens alongside. You can experiment with different herbs, coming up with a combo that pleases your palate.

YIELD: 8 SERVINGS

1 tablespoon cumin seeds

2 teaspoons fennel seeds

1 teaspoon red pepper flakes

3 garlic cloves, minced

2 teaspoons grated orange or lemon zest

1½ to 2 cups extra-virgin olive oil

2 cups (about 10 ounces) mixed Greek olives, rinsed and drained

8 ounces feta cheese, cut into ½-inch cubes

½ cup mixed minced fresh herbs (such as basil, cilantro, oregano, and parsley)

1 baguette, sliced

Place the cumin seeds, fennel seeds, and red pepper flakes in a small skillet set over medium-high heat. Shake the skillet gently until the spices are fragrant, about 1 minute. Transfer to a medium-sized bowl. Add the garlic, orange zest, and 1½ cups of the oil and stir to combine. Mix in the olives. Gently stir in the feta. If necessary, add additional oil to cover the olives and cheese. Cover with plastic wrap and refrigerate for 3 days and up to 1 week.

Return the olives to room temperature. Stir in the herbs. Serve with baguette slices.

Note: You can often find 10-ounce packages of Greek olive medley in the refrigerated section of Trader Joe's or at a green or Middle Eastern market.

Fig and Blue Cheese Crostini for Two Seasons

This combo is so good, I have two versions—one for summer when abundant fresh figs go well with Italian blue cheese, and one for winter using port-stewed dried figs and English Stilton.

YIELD: 8 CROSTINI

8 baguette slices, about ⅓-inch thick
    and 4 inches long

Summer

3 ounces creamy gorgonzola cheese,
    crumbled (about ¾ cup)
4 small ripe figs, thinly sliced

Winter

½ cup (about 2 ounces)
    thinly sliced dried Mission figs
½ cup ruby port
3 ounces Stilton cheese, crumbled
    (about ¾ cup)
Pepper

Lightly toast the baguette slices.

In summer: Preheat the broiler or toaster oven. Arrange the toasted baguette slices on a small baking sheet. Top each one with gorgonzola, dividing evenly. Arrange the fig slices atop the cheese, dividing evenly. Broil the crostini until the cheese melts and bubbles along the edges, about 3 minutes.

In winter: Combine the figs and the port in a heavy, small saucepan set over medium-low heat. Simmer until almost all the liquid is gone, about 10 minutes.

Preheat the broiler or toaster oven. Top each crostini with Stilton, dividing evenly. Broil the crostini until the cheese melts and bubbles, about 2 minutes. Top with the figs, dividing evenly. Season with pepper and serve.

Goat Cheese and Poblano Pepita Pesto Quesadillas

Nutty, slightly piquant pesto melds deliciously with creamy goat cheese and earthy corn tortillas in this tasty dish. This recipe makes a lot of food, so it's great for entertaining. You can, of course, make less and freeze any leftover pesto. Or thin it with cream and use it as a sauce for sautéed chicken breasts (similar to Mexican *Pipian*, or pumpkin seed sauce). I like to serve these hot off the griddle with shots of Tequila and Sangrita chasers (page 48). Pepitas are the tender green interior of pumpkin seeds—find them at health-food stores.

YIELD: 2 DOZEN QUESADILLAS

Pesto

1 poblano chile

1 cup pepitas (raw green pumpkin seeds)

1 cup coarsely chopped cilantro

1 large green onion, cut into 2-inch pieces

2 garlic cloves

2 tablespoons extra-virgin olive oil

Salt

Quesadillas

24 (6-inch) corn tortillas

12 ounces soft fresh goat cheese

To make the pesto: Char the chile over a gas flame or under a broiler until it is blackened and charred on all sides. Transfer to a bowl and cover with plastic wrap, allowing the chile to steam while it cools. Peel, seed, and stem the chile.

Combine the chile, pepitas, cilantro, green onion, garlic, and olive oil in the bowl of a food processor. Process until the mixture is finely chopped. Add ½ cup of water and blend until smooth. Season with salt. *(The pesto can be prepared up to 4 days ahead. Transfer the pesto to an airtight container and refrigerate.)*

To make the quesadillas: Heat a griddle or large iron skillet over medium-high heat. Working in batches, heat the tortillas on the griddle until they are warm and pliable, about 2 to 3 minutes. Spread about 1 tablespoon of the pesto over half of each tortilla and sprinkle with about 1 tablespoon of goat cheese. Fold the tortillas in half, enclosing the cheese and pesto. Cook the quesadillas on the griddle until the cheese is very soft and the pesto is hot, about 1 to 2 minutes per side. Transfer the quesadillas to a cutting board, cut them in half, and serve.

Variation: For a buffet-style appetizer, spread the pesto evenly over the bottom of an ovenproof gratin or baking dish. Coarsely crumble the goat cheese over the pesto and sprinkle with 2 tablespoons pepitas. Bake the queso fundido (Spanish for "melted cheese") in a preheated 350°F. oven until the cheese melts, the pesto is hot, and the mixture is beginning to brown at the edges, about 30 minutes. Serve with warm tortillas, tortilla chips, or baguette slices.

Deviled Eggs
with Chive and Tarragon

I take a simple approach to deviled eggs, enhancing the rich flavor of my backyard eggs with fresh herbs.

YIELD: 12

6 large eggs
3 tablespoons sour cream
2 tablespoons mayonnaise, preferably organic
2 teaspoons Dijon mustard
1 tablespoon snipped fresh chives
1 tablespoon minced fresh tarragon
Salt
Pink peppercorns, cracked, or black pepper

Cover the eggs with water in a large saucepan and bring to a gentle simmer. Simmer the eggs slowly for 5 minutes. Remove the eggs from the heat, cover, and let stand for 5 minutes. Rinse with cold water to cool. Refrigerate the eggs until well chilled.

Peel the eggs and carefully cut them in half lengthwise. Remove the yolks and transfer them to a medium-sized bowl. Set the whites aside. Stir the yolks with a fork, breaking them into bits. Add the sour cream, mayonnaise, and mustard and stir until smooth. Mix in the chives and tarragon and season with salt to taste. Spoon the yolk mixture into the egg whites, dividing evenly. Sprinkle the tops with pink peppercorns. Serve, or chill and serve within 3 hours.

Citrus Blossom Cocktail

This beverage combines the gorgeous fragrance of an orange blossom with the punch of a serious drink.

YIELD: 1 SERVING

3 tablespoons vodka
2 tablespoons Cointreau
2 tablespoons fresh orange juice
1 tablespoon fresh Meyer lemon or lemon juice
¼ teaspoon angostura bitters
1 drop orange-flower water
1 orange twist
Ice

Combine the vodka, Cointreau, orange juice, lemon juice, bitters, and flower water in a cocktail shaker. Run the orange twist around the edge of a stemmed martini glass and add it to the shaker. Add ice and shake. Strain into the glass and enjoy.

Photo on page 49

Tequila and Sangrita

After numerous trips to Mexico, I've acquired a taste for premium tequila. I like to sip the spirit straight followed by sangrita, the traditional chaser. Sangrita, which means "little blood," is a concoction of citrus, chile, and salt, and sometimes tomato juice and grenadine. I developed this version using citrus and my homemade version of grenadine—reduced pomegranate juice.

YIELD: 2½ CUPS SANGRITA, ABOUT 10 SHOTS

2 cups pure pomegranate juice
2 cups fresh orange juice
¼ cup fresh lime juice
1 teaspoon salt
½ teaspoon cayenne pepper
Tequila

Simmer the pomegranate juice over medium-low heat in a heavy, large saucepan until reduced to ½ cup, about 10 minutes. Transfer to a pitcher and cool. Add the orange and lime juices, the salt, and cayenne pepper to the pitcher and mix well. Refrigerate the sangrita until well chilled, about 2 hours. *(The sangrita can be prepared 4 days ahead; cover and refrigerate.)*

Fill some shot glasses with tequila. Stir the sangrita and pour into separate shot glasses and serve.

Mojitos

Mint grows like a weed in my front yard, back yard, and even in my potted orchids. My version of the classic Cuban cocktail is sweetened with lime sugar.

YIELD: ABOUT 5 TABLESPOONS LIME SUGAR; 1 MOJITO

Lime Sugar
¼ cup sugar
½ teaspoon finely grated lime zest

Mojito
1 tablespoon fresh mint leaves
¼ cup golden rum
1 tablespoon fresh lime juice
Ice
¼ cup soda water

To make the lime sugar: Combine the sugar and lime zest in a small bowl. Use your fingertips to rub the zest into the sugar to release the oils.

To make the mojitos: Combine the mint and 1 tablespoon lime sugar in a glass. Using a wooden pestle or muddler, muddle the mint and sugar. Add the rum and lime juice and stir briefly to dissolve the sugar. Fill the glass with ice. Add the soda water to the glass, stir gently, and serve.

Photo on page 49

SOUPS

French Lentil and Sausage Soup with Swiss Chard

This hearty soup-stew combines the rich flavors of Southern France. Pair it with a crusty baguette, and you've got a satisfying one-dish supper. French lentils are smaller than regular lentils. They are dark green, hold their shape when tender, and have a slight peppery flavor. If your market doesn't carry them, you can find them online. Sometimes vacuum-sealed steamed French lentils are available at specialty food stores. You can use them in this soup if you want to cut down on cooking time—just simmer them along with the carrots until the carrots are tender.

YIELD: 6 SERVINGS

2 tablespoons olive oil
1 large onion, chopped
1 pound smoked sausage, preferably duck
6 garlic cloves, sliced
1½ cups dried French green lentils
1 teaspoon herbes de Provence
4 large carrots (about 12 ounces), peeled and cut into ¼-inch-thick rounds
Kosher salt
1 bunch Swiss chard, about 1 pound
Pepper

Heat the olive oil in a heavy, large pot over medium heat. Add the onion and sauté until golden, about 10 minutes.

Cut the sausage into ½-inch rounds. Add to the pot and cook, stirring frequently, until the sausage is lightly browned, about 5 minutes. Add the garlic and cook 1 minute. Add the lentils, 7 cups water, and the herbes de Provence, and simmer for 10 minutes. Add the carrots and a good sprinkle of salt. Simmer until the lentils are very tender and the broth is slightly thick, about 1 hour.

Remove the tough stems from the chard and cut it crosswise into 2-inch-thick strips. Stir in the chard and simmer just until it wilts, about 3 minutes. Season the soup to taste with salt and pepper.

Vietnamese Beef Pho with Star Anise and Aromatic Herbs

When making this richly flavored soup, use either homemade beef broth, purchased low-salt beef broth, or the Better than Bouillon brand base. Serve it in large bowls for lunch or dinner. Let your guests garnish their soup with the aromatic herbs of their choice. Thai basil has smaller leaves, reddish stems, and a stronger, almost licorice flavor—if you can't find it, use the more familiar sweet basil.

YIELD: 6 SERVINGS

2 quarts beef broth

1¼ pounds beef neck or shank bones

8 green onions

2-inch piece fresh ginger, sliced

3 large whole star anise

Salt and pepper

1 (6-ounce) package dried rice stick noodles (*maifun*)

2 cups mung bean sprouts

1 bunch cilantro, trimmed

1 bunch mint, trimmed

1 bunch basil (preferably Thai), trimmed

2 serrano chiles, thinly sliced

Lime wedges

¾ pound rib-eye steak, fat trimmed, *very* thinly sliced

Combine the beef broth, bones, 4 of the green onions, the ginger, and star anise in a heavy, large pot. Bring the broth to a boil. Reduce the heat, cover, and simmer the broth very gently for 3 hours. Remove the bones and onions from the broth and discard them. Season the broth to taste with salt and pepper. (*Can be prepared to this point up to 4 days ahead. Cool, cover, and refrigerate.*)

Soak the noodles for 3 minutes in a bowl filled with enough hot water to cover. Drain the noodles.

Slice the 4 remaining green onions and place on a platter. Arrange the bean sprouts, cilantro, mint, basil, chiles, and lime wedges on the same platter.

Bring the broth to a boil over medium-high heat. Add the noodles and cook until tender, about 2 minutes. Add the steak slices and simmer until they are just cooked, about 1 minute. Ladle the soup into bowls. Pass the condiments separately.

Star Anise: *Dried star anise are hard, reddish-brown, star-shaped pods. The pods are the fruit of a small magnolia that is native to China. It adds a sweet, spicy, licorice-like flavor to sweets and savories. It is a key ingredient in Chinese five-spice powder.*

Butternut Squash Soup
with Prosciutto and Rosemary

Prosciutto gives this smooth fall soup full flavor, and rosemary balances the sweetness of the squash and the saltiness of the ham. Some markets carry 1-pound packages of cubed butternut squash—you can use two packages for this recipe to cut down on prep time.

YIELD: 4 TO 6 SERVINGS

2 tablespoons olive oil

1 medium onion, sliced

2 tablespoons diced prosciutto

4 garlic cloves

2 small butternut squash (about 1¾ to 2 pounds each), peeled, seeded, and cubed

5 cups chicken broth, plus more if needed

½ teaspoon minced fresh rosemary

Salt and pepper

Heat the olive oil in a heavy, large pot over medium heat. Add the onion and sauté until tender, about 8 minutes. Stir in the prosciutto and garlic; sauté for 1 minute. Add the squash and broth. Cover and simmer until the squash is very tender, about 15 minutes.

Using an immersion or standard blender, purée the soup (in batches, if necessary). Add the rosemary, season with salt and pepper to taste, and simmer for 5 minutes to blend the flavors, thinning the soup with additional broth if necessary. Ladle into bowls and serve. *(Can be prepared up to 3 days ahead. Cool, cover, and refrigerate. Reheat, stirring, over medium heat until warmed through.)*

Variation: *To make a vegetarian version of this soup, leave out the ham and substitute apple juice or vegetable broth for the chicken broth.*

Sopa de Limón

"Lime soup" is actually a rich chicken soup topped with crisp tortilla strips, avocados, tomatoes, green onions, and cilantro. I like to add a lime leaf to the broth to lend a floral lime flavor.

YIELD: 6 SERVINGS

Soup

2 tablespoons olive oil

6 garlic cloves, minced

1 teaspoon cumin seeds

4 cups chicken broth

3 large chicken breast halves with skin and bones

1 tablespoon chopped fresh oregano,
  or 1 teaspoon dried

1 bay leaf, preferably fresh

1 kaffir lime leaf, optional

½ cup corn oil

6 corn tortillas, cut into ½-inch-thick strips

⅓ cup fresh lime juice

Salt

Toppings

2 avocados, peeled, pitted, and diced

3 tomatoes, chopped

3 green onions, sliced

1 bunch cilantro, chopped

3 jalapeño chiles, sliced into rounds

Lime wedges

Heat the olive oil in a heavy, large saucepan over medium heat. Add the garlic and cumin seeds and sauté until fragrant, about 1 minute. Add the broth, chicken, oregano, bay leaf, lime leaf, and 4 cups water. Cover and simmer gently until the chicken is cooked through, about 35 minutes. Cool. (*Can be prepared to this point up to 2 days ahead. Cover and refrigerate.*)

Shred the chicken and return the meat to the broth; discard the bones and skin.

Heat the corn oil in a heavy, large iron skillet or shallow saucepan over medium-high heat. Fry the tortilla strips in batches until crisp. Drain on paper towels. (*The tortilla strips can be prepared several hours ahead; keep at room temperature.*)

Return the soup to a simmer. Add the lime juice and season with salt to taste. Ladle the soup into shallow bowls. Top the soup with avocado, tomato, green onion, cilantro, and tortilla strips. Serve, passing the jalapeño slices and lime wedges separately.

Cauliflower and Parsnip Soup with Currant and Pine Nut Garnish

Parsnips lend both sweetness and creaminess to cauliflower soup. Pine nuts are the edible seeds of the piñon pine. They give the unique topping a bit of crunch.

YIELD: 6 TO 8 SERVINGS

Soup

2 tablespoons extra-virgin olive oil

1 large onion, coarsely chopped

1 cauliflower, trimmed and broken
   into florets

1 pound parsnips, peeled, trimmed,
   and sliced

1 bay leaf, preferably fresh

Salt

Topping

½ cup pine nuts, toasted

¼ cup currants

1 tablespoon chopped fresh thyme

1 tablespoon extra-virgin olive oil

Salt and pepper

Tip: Because of the high oil content in pine nuts, they burn very easily. I have unintentionally burned the expensive little nuts in the oven so many times that now I toast them in a skillet where I can keep my eyes on them. Stir pine nuts constantly over medium heat until they are golden brown. Transfer them to a bowl as soon as they are toasted so they don't continue to brown in the skillet.

To make the soup: Heat the oil in a heavy, large saucepan or pot over medium heat. Add the onion, cover, and cook until the onion is tender and just beginning to turn golden, about 8 minutes. Add the cauliflower, parsnips, bay leaf, and 8 cups water. Bring to a boil. Cover and simmer over low heat until the vegetables are very tender, about 30 minutes.

Cool slightly and remove the bay leaf. Using an immersion or standard blender, purée the soup (in batches, if necessary) until smooth. Season with salt to taste. *(Can be prepared 3 days ahead. Cool, cover, and refrigerate. Reheat, stirring over medium heat.)*

To make the topping: Mix the pine nuts, currants, thyme, and oil in a small bowl. Season the garnish to taste with salt and pepper.

To serve, ladle the soup into bowls and top with a spoonful of the garnish.

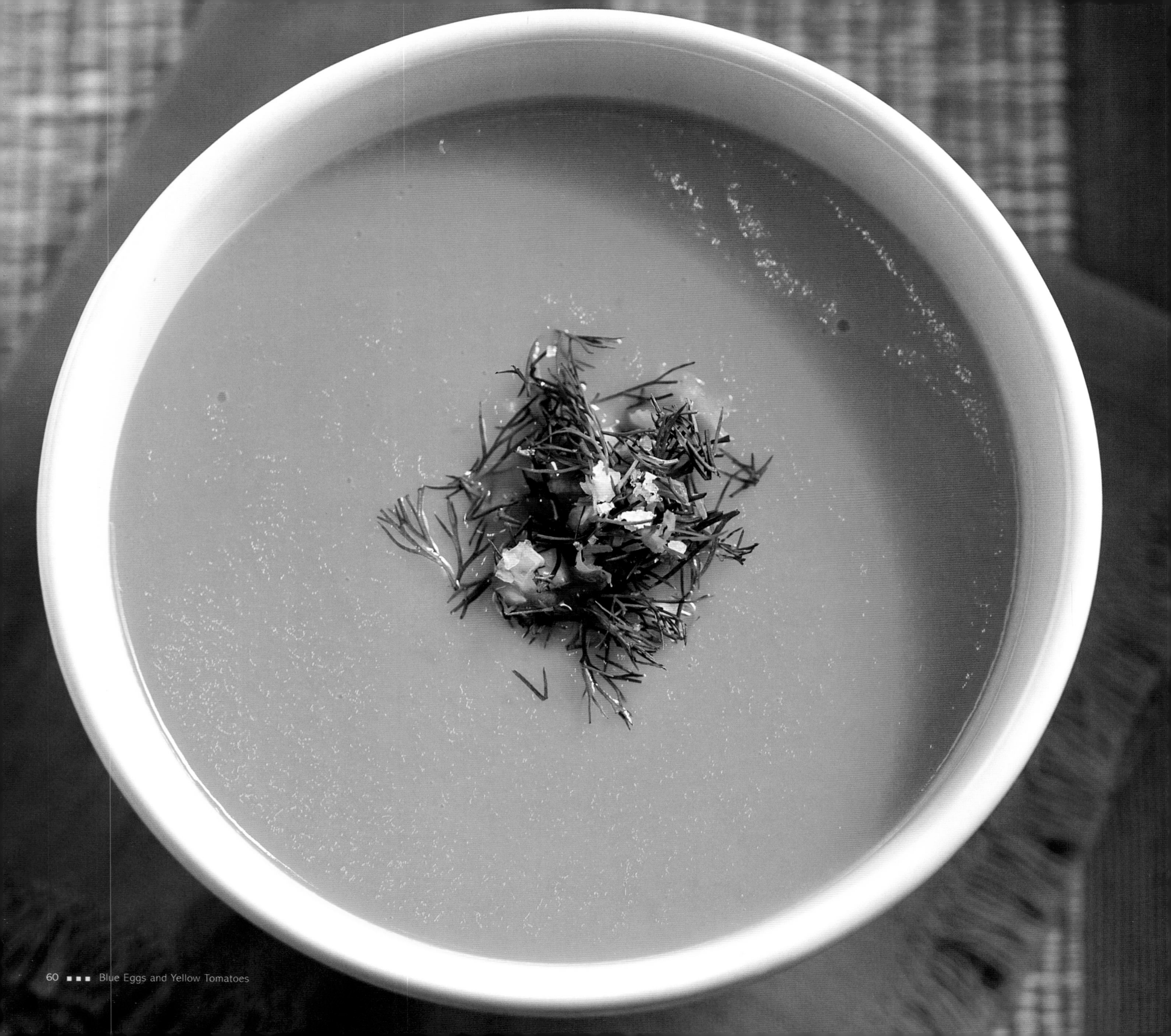

Sweet Carrot Soup with Dill Gremolata

I like to use Nantes carrots for this soup because they are very sweet and have excellent carrot flavor when cooked. You will find this French variety at farmers' markets and at some specialty food stores—they are very brittle, so they may be sold in bags of bits and pieces. Nantes carrots are also a good carrot to grow. I find a little scrubbing is all they need. If you substitute other carrots, you may want to peel them. Gremolata is the traditional citrus zest, garlic, and parsley garnish for osso buco (Italian stewed veal shanks). This dill version is great in this soup.

YIELD: 4 TO 6 SERVINGS

Soup

3 tablespoons unsalted butter

½ cup sliced shallots

2 pounds Nantes carrots or other
    sweet carrots

1 bay leaf, preferably fresh

Salt

Gremolata

2 tablespoons minced fresh dill

1 tablespoon minced shallot

½ teaspoon finely grated orange zest

¼ teaspoon fleur de sel

To make the soup: Melt the butter in a heavy, very large saucepan over medium heat. Add the shallots and sauté until tender, about 3 minutes. Cut the carrots into ½-inch rounds, add them to the pan, and stir briefly to coat with butter. Add 4 cups water and the bay leaf and bring to a boil. Cover and simmer over low heat until the carrots are very tender, about 25 minutes.

Remove the bay leaf and discard. Using an immersion or standard blender, purée the soup (in batches, if necessary). Season with salt to taste. (*Can be prepared up to 2 days ahead. Cool, cover, and refrigerate. Reheat, stirring over medium heat.*)

To make the gremolata: Combine all the ingredients in a small bowl.

To serve, ladle the soup into bowls and sprinkle with the gremolata.

Corn Chowder with Applewood-Smoked Bacon

Corn chowder is an excellent way to enjoy the sweet corn that is available at farmers' markets in the summertime. Adding potatoes makes the chowder more substantial, while chiles add heat, and bacon adds smokiness. This soup makes a good, easy dinner when paired with some quesadillas. You can use frozen corn kernels when corn is not in season.

YIELD: 4 SERVINGS

1 poblano chile
4 slices applewood-smoked bacon, cut crosswise into ¼-inch pieces
1 onion, diced
2 garlic cloves, minced
1 tablespoon chopped fresh oregano
3½ cups white or yellow corn kernels (about 4 ears) or 16 ounces frozen corn
2 cups chicken broth
1 cup milk
½ pound new potatoes, diced
Salt and pepper

Char the chile over a gas flame or under a broiler until it is blackened and charred on all sides. Transfer the chile to a bowl, cover with plastic wrap, and allow it to steam while cooling. Peel, seed, stem, and dice the chile. (*Can be prepared up to 2 days ahead. Cover and refrigerate.*)

Cook the bacon in a heavy, large saucepan over medium heat until it is almost crisp and the fat is rendered, about 7 minutes. Pour off some of the fat (leaving about 1 tablespoon) and add the onion. Cover and cook until the onion is tender, stirring occasionally, about 10 minutes. Stir in the garlic and oregano, and then the corn. Add the broth, milk, and potatoes, and bring to a simmer. Cover and cook over low heat until the potatoes are tender, about 10 minutes. Add the poblano chile and simmer for 5 minutes to blend the flavors. Season with salt and pepper. Ladle the soup into bowls and serve.

Note: *This is a chunky soup. If you prefer a creamy texture, purée 2 cups of the soup and return it to the pot, or partially purée the soup using an immersion blender.*

Curried Yellow Split Pea Soup with Mint Yogurt

I like to eat a bowl of this Indian and vegetarian version of split pea soup for lunch. Cilantro can be added in addition to or in place of the mint.

YIELD: 6 SERVINGS

Soup

16 ounces (about 2 cups) yellow split peas

3 tablespoons unsalted butter

1 large onion, chopped

4 garlic cloves, chopped

2 teaspoons curry powder

½ teaspoon ground turmeric

3 carrots, peeled

2 teaspoons kosher salt

Salt and pepper

Topping

1 cup plain yogurt

¼ cup coarsely chopped mint, lightly packed

To make the soup: Cover the peas with enough hot water to cover by 1 inch in a large bowl. Let stand for 1 hour.

Heat the butter in a heavy, large saucepan over medium heat. Add the onion and sauté until translucent, about 5 minutes. Add the garlic, curry, and turmeric, and stir for 1 minute. Drain the peas and add them to the saucepan along with 7 cups water, the carrots, and salt. Bring to a boil. Reduce the heat to very low, cover, and simmer until the peas are very tender and begin to fall apart, about 1 hour.

Using an immersion or standard blender, purée the soup (in batches, if necessary) until smooth. Season with salt and pepper to taste.

To make the topping: Stir the yogurt and mint together in a small bowl; season with salt and pepper to taste.

To serve, ladle the soup into bowls and top with a spoonful of mint yogurt.

My favorite yogurt is European Style, Organic, Plain Whole Milk Yogurt from the Straus Family Creamery, based in California and available in the western and southwestern states. The yogurt is smooth, with that perfect sweet-sour milk flavor. The creamery has a website—www.strausfamilycreamery.com—where you can learn about the cows, or their manure, which creates the electricity that runs the creamery.

Potato Soup with Sage and Migas

You've got to love a cuisine in which breadcrumbs fried in olive oil is a popular dish. The dish called *migas*—"crumbs" in Spanish—originated in the Extremadura region of Spain, where bread is often sautéed with a bit of Serrano ham and sprinkled with smoked paprika. My simplified version makes this soup special. For the breadcrumbs, I like to use day-old rustic bread torn into ¼- to ½-inch pieces.

YIELD: 4 TO 6 SERVINGS

Soup

2 pounds Yukon gold potatoes,
  peeled and cut into 2-inch pieces

5 to 6 cups chicken broth

6 garlic cloves

6 sage leaves, coarsely chopped

Salt and pepper

Migas

2 tablespoons extra-virgin olive oil

1 tablespoon unsalted butter

6 sage leaves, coarsely chopped

2 cups large fresh breadcrumbs

To make the soup: Bring the potatoes, 5 cups of the broth, the garlic, and sage to a boil in a heavy, large saucepan. Simmer, partially covered, over medium-low heat until the potatoes are very tender and beginning to fall apart, about 20 minutes.

Using an immersion or standard blender, purée the soup (in batches, if necessary) until smooth. Season with salt and pepper to taste. (*Can be prepared to this point up to 3 days ahead. Cool, cover, and refrigerate. Reheat, stirring over medium heat.*)

To make the migas: Heat the olive oil and butter in a heavy, medium-sized saucepan over medium heat. Add the sage and the breadcrumbs to the skillet and sauté until the breadcrumbs are golden brown, about 5 minutes.

To serve, ladle the soup into bowls and top with the migas.

Beef Barley Soup

Wild mushrooms give this rich, comforting soup bold flavor. The best beef stew meat is from the chuck. If your butcher doesn't have stew meat, buy a 1½-pound piece of boneless chuck and cut it into 1- to 2-inch cubes. Dried porcini mushrooms are available at Italian markets, specialty food stores, and many supermarkets.

YIELD: ABOUT 8 SERVINGS

2 tablespoons olive oil
12 ounces (about 7 cups) assorted fresh wild mushrooms
    (such as shiitake, crimini, and oyster), sliced
1 large onion, chopped
1½ pounds beef stew meat
4 garlic cloves, chopped
½ cup dried porcini mushrooms, broken into pieces
4 cups beef broth
½ pound parsnips, peeled and diced
½ pound carrots, peeled and diced
¾ cup pearl barley
3 tablespoons chopped fresh thyme or 2 tablespoons dried
Salt and pepper

Heat the oil in a heavy, large pot over medium-high heat. Add the fresh mushrooms and onions. Sauté until the mushrooms brown, about 18 minutes.

Add the beef and garlic and cook until the beef browns, about 6 minutes. Add 3 cups water, the porcini mushrooms, and the remaining ingredients and bring to a boil. Reduce the heat to medium-low. Cover and simmer until the meat is very tender, about 1½ hours.

Season the soup to taste with salt and pepper. *(Can be made up to 3 days ahead. Cool slightly at room temperature. Cover and refrigerate. Reheat over medium heat.)*

Gazpacho

Gazpacho is a classic Andalusian soup. This recipe is fairly traditional—I've added a cucumber because I like the cooling flavor it lends. Don't bother making this Spanish soup unless you are using the best tomatoes, preferably homegrown or really ripe ones from the farmers' market. Serve this for lunch or as a light supper with a salad and some thinly sliced Serrano ham.

YIELD: 6 TO 8 SERVINGS

3 pounds ripe tomatoes
2 (½-inch-thick) slices crusty white bread
1 large cucumber, peeled, seeded, and chopped
3 tablespoons extra-virgin olive oil, plus additional for drizzling
2 tablespoons sherry wine vinegar
2 garlic cloves
1 teaspoon chopped fresh oregano
Salt and pepper
1 green bell pepper, finely diced

Fill a large bowl with ice water and set it next to your stove. Bring a medium-sized saucepan of water to a boil. Using a small knife, cut a shallow "x" into the smooth bottoms of the tomatoes. Drop the tomatoes, about 3 at a time, into the boiling water for about 20 seconds. Using a slotted spoon, transfer the tomatoes to the ice water. Repeat with the remaining tomatoes.

Peel the tomatoes and discard the peel. Working over a bowl to catch the seeds and juices, quarter the tomatoes and remove the seeds. Return the tomato quarters to the ice water. Strain the juice from the seeds into a large bowl.

Cut the bread into ½-inch cubes (you should have about 1 cup) and add them, plus 1 cup of the ice water, to the tomato juice. Let the mixture stand for 20 minutes to soften the bread.

Add the tomatoes, cucumber, olive oil, vinegar, garlic, and oregano to the bread mixture. Using an immersion or standard blender, purée the mixture (in batches, if necessary) until smooth. Season with salt and pepper. Chill for at least 3 hours.

To serve, ladle the soup into bowls and garnish with bell pepper and a drizzle of olive oil.

Chilled Cucumber Soup

This soup is a refreshing prelude to a summer dinner. Garnish it with the topping that suits your menu or mood.

YIELD: 4 SERVINGS

1 green onion
1 cup lowfat buttermilk, chilled
⅓ cup sour cream
½ garlic clove
2¼ pounds (about 3 large) cucumbers, peeled, seeded,
  and cut into 2-inch pieces
Salt

Cut the white and pale-green parts from the green onion and place in a blender. Thinly slice the remaining dark-green part, cover with plastic wrap, and refrigerate. Add the buttermilk, sour cream, garlic, and half the cucumbers to the blender and purée. Add the remaining cucumbers and purée until smooth. Season with salt to taste. Cover and refrigerate until well chilled.

To serve, ladle the soup into bowls and garnish with the reserved green onion and your choice of toppings.

Toasted Fennel and Cumin Seeds and Cilantro Topping

1 teaspoon fennel seeds
1 teaspoon cumin seeds
2 tablespoons chopped fresh cilantro

Toast the fennel and cumin seeds in a heavy, small skillet over medium-high heat until golden and fragrant. Remove the skillet from the heat and set aside to cool. Sprinkle the seeds and cilantro over the soup.

Dill and Sour Cream Topping

Sour cream
Pepper
2 tablespoons chopped fresh dill

Spoon a small dollop of sour cream into each bowl of soup, sprinkle lightly with pepper, and top with dill.

Tomato and Mint Topping

1 small tomato, seeded and finely diced
2 tablespoons chopped fresh mint
Pepper

Sprinkle the tomato, mint, and pepper over the soup and serve.

Creamy Black Bean Soup with Crema Mexicana and Ancho Chiles

This velvety-smooth soup reminds me of the dark, robustly flavored black bean dishes of Oaxaca in southern Mexico. Ancho chiles are dried poblano peppers. They have a sweet, earthy flavor with moderate heat. Be sure to use chiles that are freshly dried and still pliable. Crema Mexicana is similar to crème fraîche and is sometimes labeled "pourable table cream." You can find the chiles and crema at Mexican markets, specialty food stores, and at some supermarkets.

YIELD: 6 TO 8 SERVINGS

6 cups Black Beans with Orange and Chipotle (page 236)
2 dried ancho chiles, stemmed and seeded
½ cup olive oil
Crema Mexicana or sour cream
Chopped fresh cilantro

Prepare the black beans as directed in the recipe.

Combine the beans and 3 cups water in a heavy, large saucepan. Using an immersion or standard blender, purée the beans (in batches, if necessary) until smooth. The soup should be somewhat thick. Add more water to thin the soup if necessary. (*Can be prepared to this point up to 2 days ahead. Cool, cover, and refrigerate.*)

Cut the chiles into thin strips. Heat the olive oil in a heavy, medium-sized skillet over medium heat. Add half the chile strips and cook until they darken slightly (do not let them burn), about 30 seconds to 1 minute. Transfer the chiles to a plate and let them cool (they should be crisp). Repeat with the remaining strips. (*Can be prepared up to 2 days ahead. Cover and store at room temperature.*)

Heat the soup over medium heat.

To serve, ladle the soup into bowl. Drizzle a spoonful of Crema Mexicana over the top of the soup and garnish with ancho chile strips and cilantro.

$\sim$

Tip: *Don't discard the olive oil from the fried chile strips. You can use this mild chile oil to brush over fish before grilling or to sauté vegetables. It adds great flavor.*

Salads

Green Apple, Almond, and Manchego Salad

This crisp and flavorful salad is really good when paired with a glass of chilled fino sherry. If you accompany the salad with some bread and sliced Spanish chorizo, it's an excellent light meal.

YIELD: 4 SERVINGS

Dressing

1 tablespoon white balsamic vinegar

2 teaspoons sherry wine vinegar

1 tablespoon minced shallot

3 tablespoons extra-virgin olive oil

Salt

Salad

8 butterhead lettuce leaves

4 cups mâche rosettes or butterhead lettuce, torn into bite-sized pieces, lightly packed

1 medium Granny Smith apple, cut into matchstick-sized strips

2 ounces Manchego cheese, cut into strips

¼ cup coarsely chopped salted almonds, preferably Marcona almonds, roasted

To make the dressing: Combine both the vinegars and the shallot in a small bowl. Whisk in the oil and season with salt to taste.

To make the salad: Line each of four plates with two butterhead lettuce leaves. Drizzle with a small amount of the vinaigrette. Combine the mâche, apple, cheese, and almonds in a large bowl. Add enough of the vinaigrette to coat the salad lightly and toss well. Divide the salad evenly among the plates, on top of the lettuce.

Marcona almonds are Spanish almonds. They are flatter than regular almonds, super crunchy, and have a sweet flavor. They're really delicious, but they're also hard to find and a bit pricey. California almonds are delicious too, so don't hesitate to use them.

Orange, Red Onion, and Date Salad

Peppery greens combine with juicy oranges and sweet dates in this pretty "platter salad." You can double or triple the salad for entertaining.

YIELD: 6 TO 8 SERVINGS

Salad

4 oranges

4 cups watercress, trimmed,
   lightly packed

4 cups baby frisée, torn into bite-sized
   pieces, lightly packed

½ small red onion,
   sliced into very thin rounds

8 pitted Deglet Noor dates,
   sliced into rounds

Dressing

2 tablespoons white balsamic vinegar

1 teaspoon curry powder

2 tablespoons grapeseed oil

Salt

To make the salad: Use a long sharp knife to cut the peel and white pith from the oranges. Cut in between the membranes to release the orange segments. Arrange the watercress and frisée on a large platter. Top with the orange segments, onion, and dates in a decorative manor.

To make the dressing: Whisk the vinegar and curry powder together in a small bowl. Whisk in the oil and season generously with salt.

   Drizzle the dressing over the salad and serve.

Frisée Salad with Fried Egg and Applewood-Smoked Bacon

This version of the French *Salade Lyonnaise* is, for me, the ultimate comfort dish. I enjoy this salad as a late breakfast, lunch, or for dinner with a glass of Viognier. The recipe below is for a single serving, but it can easily be multiplied to please many. Baby frisée is a fine, feathery lettuce that is a member of the endive family. The slightly bitter flavor is well suited to the salty bacon and creamy egg.

YIELD: 1 SERVING

Dressing

1 tablespoon finely chopped shallot

2 teaspoons toasted walnut oil

1½ teaspoons best-quality, oak-aged red wine
    vinegar, such as *vinaigre de banyuls*

Sea salt and pepper

Salad

2 slices applewood-smoked uncured
    or dry-cured bacon, cut into ½-inch pieces

1 egg

2 cups baby frisée, lightly packed

Baguette, sliced

To make the dressing: Whisk together the shallot, walnut oil, and vinegar in a small bowl. Season with salt and pepper to taste.

To make the salad: Fry the bacon in a heavy, medium-sized skillet until crisp. Using a slotted spoon, transfer the bacon to a paper towel or brown bag to drain. Add ½ teaspoon bacon fat to the dressing.

Pour off most of the remaining bacon fat from the skillet. Heat the skillet over medium heat and fry the egg, turning once, about 2 to 3 minutes.

Meanwhile, toss the frisée with the bacon and dressing and transfer to a plate. Top the salad with the egg and season with salt and pepper. Serve immediately with baguette slices.

Spinach and Red Mustard Salad with Curried Dal

Dal is the Hindi word for a huge variety of dried pulses, including split peas and lentils. They are an integral part of an Indian meal. In this recipe, sprouted mung beans, which are available in the refrigerated section of health food stores, make a fresh alternative. You can substitute green mustard greens for the red, if desired. Serve this salad for lunch or with the Whole-Spice Chicken Curry on page 174.

YIELD: 4 SERVINGS

Dal

1-inch piece fresh ginger, peeled and sliced

1 jalapeño chile, stemmed and seeded

3 tablespoons grapeseed oil

2 tablespoons fresh lime juice

1 tablespoon minced cilantro

¼ teaspoon ground turmeric

Salt and pepper

1 cup sprouted mung beans

1 cup canned garbanzo beans, drained

Salad

1 tablespoon grapeseed oil

1 tablespoon fresh lime juice

¼ teaspoon ground turmeric

Salt and pepper

4 cups baby spinach leaves

1½ cups red mustard leaves,
    cut into thin strips

1 small tomato, diced

1 green onion, finely sliced

Fresh cilantro leaves

To make the dal: Combine the ginger, jalapeño, grapeseed oil, lime juice, cilantro, and turmeric in a blender and blend until smooth. Season with salt and pepper to taste. In a medium-sized bowl, combine the mung beans and garbanzo beans and add the ginger mixture. Let stand for 1 hour.

To make the salad: Whisk the grapeseed oil, lime juice, and turmeric together in a small bowl. Season with salt and pepper to taste.

Combine the spinach, red mustard, tomato, and green onion in a large shallow bowl. Toss with the dressing. Mound the dal mixture in the center. Garnish with cilantro and serve.

Green Bean, Corn, and Farro Salad

This minty salad mixes sweet corn, crisp green beans, and chewy farro, a nutty-flavored grain from Tuscany. I like to serve this fresh salad with grilled fish. With the addition of crumbled, soft, fresh goat cheese, it makes a great vegetarian entrée or accompaniment to grilled chicken.

YIELD: 6 SERVINGS

Dressing

¼ cup extra-virgin olive oil

2 tablespoons fresh lemon juice

2 tablespoons white balsamic vinegar

1 shallot, minced

1 garlic clove, minced

1 teaspoon Dijon mustard

Salad

⅔ cup semi-pearled farro or spelt berries

1 pound green beans, cut into 2-inch pieces

2 ears sweet white corn

¼ cup chopped fresh mint leaves

Salt and pepper

To make the dressing: Whisk the oil, lemon juice, vinegar, shallot, garlic, and mustard together in a large bowl.

To make the salad: Boil the farro in a medium-sized saucepan filled with salted water until just tender, about 20 to 25 minutes. Drain and let the farro cool.

Cook the green beans in a large pot of boiling salted water until crisp-tender, about 4 minutes. Drain and rinse with cold water. Pat the beans dry with a towel.

Cut the kernels from the corn cobs. Add the corn, farro, green beans, and mint to the dressing. Season with salt and pepper to taste and stir to combine. *(Can be prepared up to 1 day ahead. Cover and refrigerate.)*

Tomato and Spinach Salad with Mozzarella and Basil Dressing

The basil dressing in this salad is a touch salty, but the salt keeps the basil green and brightly flavored while also seasoning the fresh mozzarella.

YIELD: 4 SERVINGS

Dressing

¼ cup fresh basil leaves, firmly packed

1 garlic clove

½ teaspoon kosher salt

¼ cup extra-virgin olive oil

2 teaspoons balsamic vinegar

Salad

2 cups halved grape or cherry tomatoes

4 cups baby spinach leaves, lightly packed

12 ounces fresh mozzarella, sliced

To make the dressing: Chop the basil leaves together with the garlic and salt until the garlic is finely chopped and basil is almost puréed. Transfer the mixture to a small bowl and stir in the olive oil and vinegar.

To make the salad: Combine the tomatoes with 2 tablespoons of the dressing in a medium-sized bowl. Toss the spinach in a large shallow bowl with 2 tablespoons of the dressing. Arrange the mozzarella slices atop the spinach and drizzle with the remaining dressing. Spoon the tomatoes and their juices onto the center of the salad and serve.

Note: *If you're sensitive to sodium, cut the salt in the dressing back to* ¼ *teaspoon.*

Beet and Red Greens Salad with Walnuts and Maytag Blue Cheese

The earthy-sweet flavor of beets pairs really well with the rich walnuts and creamy blue cheese in this salad. You can use any combination of red lettuces here—even the readily available red leaf lettuce will be great. The beets can be roasted a few days ahead and kept on hand in the refrigerator. If you've got beets in your garden or you buy a fresh bunch from the farmers' market, reserve some of the tender leaves to add to the salad.

YIELD: 4 SERVINGS

Dressing

¼ cup minced shallot

3 tablespoons toasted walnut oil

2 tablespoons red wine vinegar

Salt and pepper

Salad

2 bunches baby beets, trimmed

Vegetable oil

8 cups greens (such as lolla rosa,
   red Belgian endive, radicchio, red butter
   lettuce, and baby beet greens),
   lightly packed

½ cup walnuts, toasted

4 ounces Maytag blue cheese, crumbled

To make the dressing: Whisk the shallot, walnut oil, and vinegar together in a small bowl. Season with salt and pepper to taste.

To make the salad: Preheat the oven to 375ºF.

Arrange the beets in the center of a sheet of aluminum foil. Drizzle them with a small amount of vegetable oil and enclose in the foil. Roast until tender, about 1 hour. Cool. (*Can be prepared up to 3 days ahead; refrigerate.*)

Peel and quarter the beets.

Toss the beets with half the dressing in a small bowl. Toss the greens with the remaining dressing in a large shallow bowl. Mound the beets in the center of the greens. Sprinkle with the walnuts and cheese and serve.

Variation: *To make this a main course salad, just add chicken. Place 4 chicken breast halves (with skin and bones) skin-side up on a small roasting pan. Brush the chicken with walnut oil and season generously with salt and pepper and 2 teaspoons minced fresh thyme. Roast the chicken with the beets until they are just cooked through, about 35 minutes. Cool completely, wrap in plastic, and refrigerate. Pull the meat from the bones and cut the chicken into slices. Arrange the chicken slices around the beets.*

Japanese Greens with Teriyaki Tofu, Edamame, and Sesame Dressing

Tahini is sesame seed paste, which you can find at many grocery stores, health food stores, and Middle Eastern markets. It adds a rich sesame flavor and creamy texture to the dressing here. Tatsoi, a baby cabbage; mizuna, a feathery green; and Japanese spinach, a large tender-leaf spinach, can all be found at farmers' and Japanese markets. They lend a Japanese accent to this vegetarian main course. If you can't find them, don't worry; the salad is equally delicious when made with Napa cabbage and baby spinach.

YIELD: 4 SERVINGS

Dressing

3 tablespoons dark sesame oil

2 tablespoons tahini

2 tablespoons seasoned rice wine vinegar

1 tablespoon soy sauce

Salad

1 ½ cups shelled edamame

2 cups tatsoi or napa cabbage leaves,
    cut into ½-inch slices

2 cups mizuna or Japanese or baby spinach,
    cut into bite-sized pieces

1 Persian or half of an English cucumber,
    cut into rounds

1 (8-ounce) package baked
    teriyaki-flavored tofu, cubed

1 green onion, thinly sliced

Toasted sesame seeds

To make the dressing: Whisk all of the ingredients in a small bowl.

To make the salad: Bring a small saucepan of salted water to a rapid boil. Add the edamame and cook until just tender, about 5 minutes. Drain and cool the edamame.

Arrange the tatsoi, mizuna, cucumber, tofu, and green onion on 4 plates. Spoon some of the dressing over each salad. Sprinkle with sesame seeds and serve.

A Persian cucumber is a small, tender cucumber that does not need to be peeled or seeded. It is more tender than an English cucumber, yet still crisp, with a sweet flavor.

Eggplant and Herb Salad with Sumac Dressing

Eggplant is a staple in the Mediterranean. Its richness is perfectly suited to this tart and lemony herb salad, which looks gorgeous. Make a meal of this dish with some hummus and pita bread.

YIELD: 4 SERVINGS

Dressing

2 tablespoons fresh lemon juice

1 large garlic clove, pressed

2 teaspoons cumin seeds, toasted

2 teaspoons ground sumac, optional

Salad

1 large (16-ounce) eggplant, thinly sliced

Extra-virgin olive oil

Salt

2 cups arugula

2 cups assorted herbs (such as basil, flat-leaf parsley, cilantro, and dill)

3 ounces feta cheese, crumbled

To make the dressing: Combine the lemon juice, garlic, cumin, and sumac in a small bowl. Whisk in $\frac{1}{4}$ cup olive oil and season the dressing to taste with salt and pepper.

To make the salad: Preheat the broiler.

Brush both sides of the eggplant slices with olive oil. Arrange the slices in one layer on a baking sheet and season with salt. Broil until browned and tender, about 4 minutes, checking frequently. Cool completely.

Arrange the eggplant slices on a platter and drizzle with half the dressing.

In a large bowl, toss the arugula and herbs with enough of the remaining dressing to season lightly. Mound the herb salad atop the eggplant and sprinkle with feta.

Ground from the berries of a shrub with the same name, sumac is a spice used in Middle Eastern cuisine. You'll often find it in shakers on the tables of Persian restaurants where it adds a tart, lemony touch to kebabs and pilaf. I love to sprinkle it on chicken before roasting.

Mexican Fruit "Gazpacho" Salad

All over Mexico, and in many parts of Los Angeles, there are fruit vendors selling an assortment of fruit—usually mango, papaya, watermelon, and cucumber—cut into spears. You can have your fruit seasoned with chile, salt, and/or lime. In the colonial city of Morelia, my family came across a stand selling *gazpacho de fruta*—diced fruit mixed with lots of chile and lime and a sprinkling of *queso añejo*. Here is a simple version of the salad. I include it at all my fiestas.

YIELD: 6 SERVINGS

1 ½ pounds Mexican papaya

¾ pounds jícama

1 large mango

1 cucumber

1 orange

3 tablespoons fresh lime juice

1 teaspoon ground chile (such as New Mexican or other medium-hot chile)

½ teaspoon kosher salt

2 tablespoons finely chopped cilantro

Peel and dice (and seed, if necessary) the papaya, jicama, mango, cucumber, and orange. Combine the diced fruit in a shallow serving dish or bowl.

Mix the lime juice, chile, and salt in a small bowl. Pour the mixture over the fruit, add the cilantro, and toss gently but well. Serve.

Jicama is a large root vegetable with thick brown skin. The white insides have the crunchy texture of apples and are slightly sweet. It's an excellent addition to crudité platters and salads. Store it in the refrigerator.

Asian Slaw with Spicy Peanut Dressing

This is a great salad to serve at a barbecue, but don't feel the rest of the food needs to be Asian inspired. Serve it with hamburgers for a fun, flavorful change.

YIELD: 8 SERVINGS

Dressing

⅓ cup natural-style creamy peanut butter

⅓ cup peanut or vegetable oil

⅓ cup seasoned rice wine vinegar

¼ cup light brown sugar, firmly packed

3 tablespoons soy sauce

2 tablespoons finely grated
   peeled fresh ginger

4 garlic cloves, pressed

Salad

½ head green cabbage, thinly sliced
   (about 6 cups)

¼ head red cabbage, thinly sliced
   (about 2 cups)

2 red bell peppers, cut into strips

2 large carrots, peeled and shredded

6 green onions, thinly sliced

½ cup chopped fresh cilantro

Salt

½ cup roasted peanuts, chopped

To make the dressing: Whisk the dressing ingredients together in a small bowl.

To make the salad: Combine the cabbages, bell peppers, carrots, green onions, and cilantro in a large bowl. Add the dressing and toss to coat. Season with salt, if necessary. *(Can be prepared several hours ahead. Cover and chill.)*

To server, transfer the slaw to a large shallow bowl and sprinkle with peanuts.

Orzo Salad with Pine Nuts, Olives, and Radicchio

Orzo, the rice-shaped pasta, makes an excellent salad as it picks up flavors so well. Here, chopped radicchio and basil add color and freshness. Take this winner to picnics or serve it at barbecues.

YIELD: 8 SERVINGS

1½ cups (about 10 ounces) orzo
⅓ cup extra-virgin olive oil
2 garlic cloves, pressed
⅓ cup pitted kalamata olives, chopped
¼ cup balsamic vinegar
1 small head radicchio, finely chopped
½ cup chopped fresh basil
½ cup pine nuts, toasted
½ cup freshly grated Parmesan cheese
Salt and pepper

Bring a large pot of salted water to a boil. Add the orzo and cook according to the package directions until tender but still firm to the bite. Drain well (do not rinse) and transfer to a large bowl. Immediately add the oil and garlic, and stir to combine. Mix in the olives and vinegar, and let the mixture stand until it cools to room temperature. (*Can be prepared to this point up to 6 hours ahead. Cover and refrigerate. Bring to room temperature before continuing.*)

Add the radicchio, basil, pine nuts, and cheese to the orzo mixture. Season with salt and pepper to taste and serve.

Carrot Salad with Green Olives and Green Onions

Carrots, olives, herbs, and a hint of orange and spice combine in this great side salad. It goes really well with the Moroccan Chicken Skewers (page 170) and couscous.

YIELD: 6 SERVINGS

Dressing

2 tablespoons extra-virgin olive oil

2 tablespoons fresh lemon juice

2 teaspoons grated orange zest

2 teaspoons ground coriander

1 teaspoon ground cumin

2 garlic cloves, pressed

Salad

1½ pounds sweet carrots, preferably organic

Salt and pepper

½ cup chopped pitted French green olives

½ cup finely sliced green onions

2 tablespoons chopped flat-leaf parsley
   or cilantro

1 tablespoon fresh lemon juice

To make the dressing: Combine the oil, lemon juice, orange zest, coriander, cumin, and garlic in a large bowl. Set aside.

To make the salad: Bring a large saucepan of generously salted water to a boil.

Peel the carrots and cut them on the diagonal into ¼-inch thick slices. Add them to the boiling water and cook until just tender (not soft), about 8 minutes. Drain well.

Add the carrots to the dressing and toss to combine. Cool and season with salt and pepper to taste. Stir in the olives and green onions. Cover and refrigerate until chilled. (*Can be prepared to this point up to 1 day ahead.*)

Stir the parsley into the salad, add the lemon juice, and adjust the seasoning, if necessary. Mound the salad onto a serving dish and serve.

Avocado and Crab Salad with Baby Greens

I use fresh tarragon in this refreshing salad, but you can substitute dill, basil, cilantro, or a combination of herbs. Serve it as a starter.

YIELD: 4 SERVINGS

Dressing

2 tablespoons fresh lemon juice

2 tablespoons minced shallot

2 teaspoons minced fresh tarragon

1½ teaspoons Dijon mustard

1 small garlic clove, pressed

¼ cup best-quality extra-virgin olive oil

Salt and pepper

Salad

2 avocados, halved and peeled

4 cups assorted baby lettuce greens

4 ounces Dungeness crabmeat

To make the dressing: Whisk the lemon juice, shallot, tarragon, mustard, and garlic together in a small bowl. Whisk in the olive oil and season with salt and pepper to taste.

To make the salad: Cut the avocado halves into slices and fan them on 4 plates. Toss the greens with 2 tablespoons of the dressing in a medium-sized bowl. Toss the crab with 1 tablespoon of the dressing in a small bowl.

Divide the lettuce evenly among the plates. Top with the crab, and drizzle the remaining dressing over the avocado slices and salad and serve.

Caesar Panzanella Salad

This salad is a cross between two favorites—the Tijuana-invented steakhouse salad and the Italian bread salad called *panzanella*. It's a wonderful side salad served with grilled or roasted chicken or it can be a light main course with the addition of a can of well-drained, olive oil–packed tuna or some hard-boiled eggs.

YIELD: 4 SERVINGS

Croutons

1 (8-ounce) loaf rustic bread

2 tablespoons extra-virgin olive oil

2 garlic cloves

Dressing

¼ cup extra-virgin olive oil

1 hard-boiled egg

3 tablespoons fresh lemon juice

4 oil-packed anchovy fillets, drained

1 teaspoon Dijon mustard

Salt and pepper

Salad

2 medium-sized tomatoes, cut into ¾-inch dice,
  or 2 cups cherry tomatoes, cut in half

½ small to medium red onion, sliced

Salt and pepper

8 cups torn romaine lettuce leaves

To make the croutons: Preheat the oven to 400°F.

Using a serrated knife, remove the short ends of the bread and discard. Cut the remainder of the loaf into ¾-inch cubes (you should have about 4 cups). Pour the olive oil in a medium-sized bowl. Using a garlic press, press the garlic into the oil. Add the bread cubes and toss well. Spread the croutons on a heavy baking pan and toast in the oven until they just begin to turn lightly golden, about 8 minutes. Cool.

To make the dressing: Combine all of the dressing ingredients in a blender and purée until smooth. Season with salt and pepper to taste.

To make the salad: Place the croutons in a medium-sized bowl. Add ⅓ cup of the dressing and the tomatoes and toss well. Let stand until the croutons begin to soften slightly, about 15 minutes.

Add the onion and season with salt and pepper to taste.

Toss the lettuce with 2 tablespoons of the dressing in a large shallow bowl. Spoon the bread salad into the center of the lettuce and serve, passing the remaining dressing separately.

Bacon, Double A, and T Sandwiches

Adding the double A—arugula and avocado—to the traditional BLT makes the perfect sandwich! Any leftover mayonnaise can be saved for later use on other sandwiches.

YIELD: 2 SANDWICHES

Mayonnaise

½ cup mayonnaise, preferably organic

2 tablespoons Dijon mustard

1 green onion, minced

1 garlic clove, minced

Sandwiches

6 slices (about 6 ounces)
   applewood-smoked bacon

4 slices country-style white
   or sourdough bread

1 avocado, sliced

1 large tomato, sliced

Salt and pepper

1 cup arugula leaves, lightly packed

To make the mayonnaise: Combine the mayonnaise ingredients in a small bowl. (*Can be made several days ahead. Cover and refrigerate.*)

To assemble the sandwiches: Cook the bacon to desired crispiness in a heavy, large skillet. Drain well.

Lightly toast the bread. Spread 2 pieces of toast with a thin layer of the mayonnaise. Top with avocado and tomato slices, dividing them evenly. Sprinkle the tomatoes with salt and pepper to taste. Arrange 3 slices of bacon atop the tomatoes. Divide the arugula between the sandwiches. Spread the remaining slices of toast with the mayonnaise and place atop the sandwiches. Press the sandwiches gently to compress. Cut each sandwich in half and serve.

Smoked Turkey and Jarlsberg Sandwiches with Spicy Mayo

This sandwich is sweet, smoky, nutty, and spicy. It holds together well, making it great to pack in lunches. Sriracha hot sauce, sometimes called "rooster sauce" because of the rooster on the bottle, is a thick hot sauce made from red jalapeño chiles. A good brand is made by the Huy Fong Company, which was started in 1980 in a small Los Angeles kitchen by a Vietnamese immigrant. The sauce quickly became hugely popular here and shows up on tables in Asian as well as Mexican restaurants. You'll love the spicy mayo I make with it.

YIELD: 4 SANDWICHES

½ cup mayonnaise, preferably organic
1 generous tablespoon Sriracha sauce
8 slices whole wheat, rye, or sourdough bread
8 ounces thinly sliced smoked turkey
6 ounces thinly sliced Jarlsberg or Swiss cheese
2 small Golden Delicious apples, thinly sliced
8 small leaves green leaf lettuce

Mix the mayonnaise and Sriracha sauce together in a small bowl. Spread the bread slices with a thin layer of the mayonnaise. Divide turkey, cheese, and apple slices evenly among 4 slices of the bread. Top each with two lettuce leaves, then the remaining bread. Cut the sandwiches in half and serve.

Broiled Iberica Cheese, Serrano Ham, and Romesco Tartines

Tartine is a fancy name for an open-faced sandwich. I like the term because it sounds "special" as in "special enough for dinner." *Saveur* magazine refers to tartines as "Knife and Fork Sandwiches," which is a good name, too. I make these tartines in my toaster oven. I'll eat a whole one for dinner with some greens dressed with sherry wine vinegar and Spanish olive oil, or I'll cut the tartines into smaller pieces and serve them as tapas with a glass of fino sherry. The romesco sauce is a wonderful condiment to roast meats. Try it with roast pork loin (see page 100).

YIELD: 2 TARTINES; 1 ⅓ CUPS SAUCE

Romesco Sauce
2 large red bell peppers
½ cup almonds, toasted
¼ cup extra-virgin olive oil
3 garlic cloves
Salt
Cayenne pepper

Tartines
2 large, thick slices country bread
2 thin slices Serrano ham or prosciutto
4 ounces thinly sliced Iberico
   or manchego cheese
1 teaspoon chopped fresh oregano,
   optional

To make the sauce: Preheat the broiler. Char the bell peppers under the broiler until blackened and charred on all sides. Transfer to a bowl and cover with plastic, allowing the peppers to steam while they cool. Peel, seed, stem, and slice the peppers.

Combine the peppers, almonds, oil, and garlic in a blender and purée until smooth. Season with salt and cayenne pepper to taste. *(Can be prepared up to 1 week ahead. Transfer to a small plastic container and refrigerate.)*

To assemble the tartines: Spread each bread slice thickly with romesco sauce and place on a baking sheet. Top with a slice of ham, then the cheese. Broil until the cheese melts and bubbles, about 3 minutes. Transfer the tartines to plates, sprinkle with the oregano, and serve.

Roast Pork Loin

Preheat the oven to 350°F. Combine 1 tablespoon minced fresh oregano, 2 minced garlic cloves and 2 teaspoons kosher salt in a small bowl. Rub a 2½-pound boneless pork loin roast with the oregano mixture (this is great if done several hours or 1 day ahead). Place the pork on a roasting pan and roast until an instant meat thermometer registers 140°F when inserted into thickest part of roast, about 1 hour 35 minutes. Let the roast stand for 10 minutes.

Smoked Whitefish and Beet Relish Tartines

Crusty organic wheat bread from a local bakery is really good in this recipe. Roasted beets are easy to make, but you can also buy cooked beets at several markets. I like smoked whitefish and trout—they are milder in flavor than smoked salmon and go excellently with the beets, watercress, and horseradish.

YIELD: 4 TARTINES

Relish

2 medium beets

1 tablespoon vegetable oil

2 green onions, finely sliced

2 teaspoons extra-virgin olive oil

1 teaspoon fresh lemon juice

Salt and pepper

Horseradish cream

⅓ cup crème fraîche or sour cream

2 tablespoons prepared horseradish

Salt and pepper

Tartines

4 slices wheat bread

4 ounces smoked whitefish or trout

16 large sprigs watercress

Tip: *I like to roast a bunch of beets all at once and keep them in the refrigerator to add to salads, sautés, and even sandwiches.*

To make the relish: Preheat the oven to 400°F.

Trim the beets and arrange them in a medium-sized baking dish. Drizzle them with the vegetable oil, cover with aluminum foil, and roast until they are tender when pierced with a small sharp knife, about 45 minutes to 1 hour. Cool. *(Can be made up to 5 days ahead of time. Cool and refrigerate in a plastic bag.)*

Finely grate the beets into a medium-sized bowl. Mix in the green onions, olive oil, and lemon juice. Season with salt and pepper to taste.

To make the horseradish cream: Mix the crème fraîche and horseradish in a small bowl. Season with salt and pepper to taste.

To assemble the tartines: Lightly toast the bread. Spread the beet relish on the toasts, dividing it evenly. Top the beet relish with smoked fish, dividing evenly. Decorate the tartines with the watercress. Drizzle about 1 generous tablespoonful of the horseradish cream over each tartine and serve.

Croque Monsieur (or Madame)

When my husband, then boyfriend, visited me in Paris while I was in cooking school, I took him to a café where they made a great croque monsieur, the French version of a grilled ham and cheese sandwich. He loved the rich, comforting, hot open-faced sandwich and hoped I would learn to make it. While the café favorite was *not* part of my culinary curriculum, I figured out how to make it. The croque madame is the same sandwich with an egg. This recipe makes enough béchamel (white sauce) for four sandwiches. I'll often make the sauce in the morning or the day before and assemble and broil the sandwiches as needed.

YIELD: ABOUT 1 CUP BÉCHAMEL; 4 SANDWICHES

Béchamel

1 tablespoon unsalted butter

2 tablespoons unbleached all-purpose flour

1 cup cold milk

1 bay leaf, preferably fresh

¼ cup grated Gruyère cheese, packed

Nutmeg

Salt and pepper

Sandwiches

4 slices *pain au levain*
   (crusty, country-style French bread)

1 cup grated Gruyère cheese, packed

¼ pound thinly sliced Black Forest ham

To make the sauce: Melt the butter in a heavy, small saucepan over medium heat. Add the flour and stir constantly for 1 minute (do not brown the flour). Add the milk all at once, then the bay leaf. Whisk to combine. Continue whisking until the sauce thickens and just comes to a boil. Remove from the heat and stir in the cheese and a light grating of fresh nutmeg. Cool slightly. Season with salt and pepper to taste. *(Can be prepared to this point up to 3 days ahead; cover and refrigerate.)*

To assemble the sandwiches: Preheat the broiler.

Lightly toast the bread. Spread each piece of toast with a layer of béchamel (about 1 generous tablespoon). Sprinkle 2 tablespoons of the cheese over each toast. Divide the ham evenly among the sandwiches, placing it atop the cheese. Spread a thick layer of the sauce over the ham and sprinkle with the remaining cheese.

Broil until the cheese melts and a few brown spots appear. Transfer the sandwiches to plates and serve with a fork and knife.

Variation: *Croque Madame. Place a lightly fried egg atop the first sprinkling of cheese. Then top with the ham, béchamel, and cheese. Be sure to broil the sandwich just until the cheese melts and the little brown spots appear—you don't want to overcook the egg.*

Tuna and Olive Bread Tartines

I like to use hearty, black olive bread for these open-faced sandwiches, but whole wheat sourdough bread tastes good as well. If you prefer, you can use the tuna salad to make traditional sandwiches. The small, tender-yet-crisp Persian cucumber does not need to be peeled or seeded. You can find them at Middle Eastern and farmers' markets and at some Trader Joe's stores. Keep the petite cucs under a damp towel as they tend to get limp quickly.

YIELD: 4 TARTINES

1 (6-ounce) can albacore tuna, drained

2 to 4 tablespoons mayonnaise, preferably organic

1 small Persian cucumber, diced, or ¼ of an English cucumber

1 large green onion, thinly sliced

2 tablespoons finely chopped fresh dill

2 tablespoons drained capers

1 tablespoon Dijon mustard

Pepper

4 slices olive bread, lightly toasted

4 slices tomato

4 romaine lettuce leaves

Combine the tuna, 2 tablespoons of the mayonnaise, the cucumber, green onion, dill, capers, and mustard together in a medium-sized bowl. Season with pepper to taste. Add the remaining 2 tablespoons of mayonnaise, if desired. Divide the tuna salad among the olive bread toasts. Top each tartine with a tomato slice and lettuce leaf and serve.

Egg Salad Tartine

Don't stir this egg salad too much—it's best chunky.

YIELD: 4 TARTINES

1 tablespoon mayonnaise, preferably organic

1 tablespoon extra-virgin olive oil

1 teaspoon Dijon mustard

1 garlic clove, pressed

4 hard-boiled eggs, quartered and sliced

½ cup diced tomato

¼ cup finely diced red onion

2 tablespoons drained capers

2 tablespoons chopped fresh basil or flat-leaf parsley

Salt and pepper

4 slices whole wheat sourdough bread

Stir the mayonnaise, olive oil, mustard, and garlic together in a medium-sized bowl. Add the eggs, tomato, onion, capers, and basil. Stir gently, just to combine. Season with salt and pepper to taste. Toast the bread lightly. Divide the salad evenly among the toast.

Whole Grain Tartines with Ricotta, Walnuts, Cherries, Honey, and Mint

I love the sweetness of fresh ricotta, and when it's paired with really good bread—as in this tartine—the best qualities of both shine through. This unique tartine is reminiscent of the Italian countryside. Try it without the greens for breakfast or for a quick snack.

YIELD: 2 TARTINES

¼ cup chopped walnuts, toasted

2 tablespoons chopped dried sour cherries

2 tablespoons honey

2 slices whole grain bread, lightly toasted

4 to 6 tablespoons fresh ricotta

1 tablespoon torn mint leaves, lightly packed

Pepper

Fleur de sel

2 cups baby greens, lightly packed

2 teaspoons toasted walnut oil

2 teaspoons cherry balsamic or balsamic vinegar

To toast nuts, preheat the oven to 375°F. Sprinkle a single layer of nuts on a small baking pan. Toast the nuts in the oven until they are golden brown and fragrant, around 8 minutes depending on the type of nut.

Variation: *This is a versatile tartine—try using chopped dried figs or pears in place of the cherries, then match the vinegar, using a fig balsamic or a pear balsamic with the greens.*

Combine the walnuts, cherries, and honey in a small bowl. Spread each slice of toast with a thick layer of ricotta. Spoon the walnut mixture over the ricotta, dividing evenly. Sprinkle with mint leaves, freshly cracked pepper, and fleur de sel.

Toss the greens with the walnut oil, vinegar, a pinch of fleur de sel, and a grating of pepper. Divide the salad and tartines between two plates and serve.

Roast Beef or Lamb Sandwiches with Red Pepper Relish

I love this sandwich when it's made with leftover grilled or roasted lamb or beef, or thin slices of deli roast beef. Making a relish and a dressing may seem like a lot of work for a sandwich, but both can be made ahead. The lavosh bread is available at Middle Eastern markets and some specialty food stores—if you make the sandwich rolls, use deli slices for best results; otherwise, all the components are great tucked into pita bread.

YIELD: MAKES 4 SANDWICHES

Relish

2 red bell peppers

3 green onions, chopped

⅓ cup minced fresh cilantro

2 tablespoons extra-virgin olive oil

1 teaspoon ground cumin

¼ teaspoon crushed red pepper flakes

Salt

Tahini Dressing

⅓ cup tahini (sesame seed paste)

2½ tablespoons fresh lemon juice

1 garlic clove, pressed

Salt

Sandwiches

2 pieces lavosh bread
    (about 18 x 12 inches)
    or 2 large pita breads

¾ pound thinly sliced roast beef or lamb

3 cups arugula or baby spinach leaves

1 cup crumbled feta cheese

To make the relish: Char the bell peppers over a gas flame or under the broiler until blackened and charred on all sides. Transfer to a bowl and cover with plastic, allowing the peppers to steam while cooling. Peel, seed, stem, and chop the peppers.

Combine the peppers with the green onions, cilantro, olive oil, cumin, and red pepper flakes in a small bowl. Season with salt to taste.

To make the dressing: Whisk the tahini, lemon juice, garlic, and ¼ cup water together in a small bowl. Season with salt to taste. *(The relish and dressing can be made up to 3 days ahead. Cover and refrigerate separately.)*

To assemble the sandwiches: Place a clean, damp dish towel on a work surface. Unfold one lavosh atop the towel. Spread half the relish over the center of the bread, forming approximately an 12 x 8-inch rectangle. Top the relish evenly with half of the sliced meat. Spread half the Tahini dressing evenly over the meat, then arrange half the arugula leaves over the dressing. Sprinkle with half the feta cheese. Fold one empty end of the bread over the sandwich fillings. Beginning at the folded end, tightly, but gently, roll the sandwich jellyroll style. Repeat with the remaining bread and fillings. Using a long sharp knife, cut each sandwich roll into 4 pieces.

If you are using pita bread, cut each round in half and spoon the relish and dressing into the four pockets, dividing evenly. Tuck the meat and arugula into the pockets, sprinkle with feta, and serve.

Note: *You can substitute a 7.4-ounce jar of fire roasted peppers, well drained, for the roasted bell peppers in this recipe.*

Artichoke, Olive, Mozzarella, and Hot Salami Sandwiches

These sandwiches are best when made a day ahead—so they're great to take on a road trip or hike. I have used this recipe to make one large sandwich on a 1-pound loaf of rustic bread, which I then serve on a cutting board with a big serrated knife.

YIELD: 4 LARGE SANDWICHES

2 (6-ounce) jars marinated artichoke hearts, drained and chopped
½ cup chopped fresh basil
2 tablespoons extra-virgin olive oil
Salt and pepper
4 panini, ciabatta, or Italian rolls (5 or 6 inches long)
12 ounces fresh water-packed mozzarella, drained and sliced
6 ounces thinly sliced hot salami
8 tablespoons green olivada (see note)

Mix the artichokes, basil, and olive oil together in a small bowl, and season with salt and pepper to taste. Cut the rolls in half lengthwise. Divide the artichoke mixture evenly among the bottom halves of the rolls. Top with mozzarella and salami. Spread the top half of each roll with 2 tablespoons of olivada and place atop the salami. Press the sandwiches lightly to compact them and wrap each one tightly in plastic wrap. Refrigerate the sandwiches for at least 4 hours and up to 1 day.

Olivada, sometimes called olive paste, can be found at Italian markets and fancy food stores. If you can't find it, purée ½ cup pitted, brine-cured green olives with 2 tablespoons extra-virgin olive oil in a food processor.

Cuban Sandwiches
with Sriracha and Mojito Mayonnaise

A Cuban sandwich—or *Cubano*—is a grilled sandwich with ham, pork loin, and cheese. This recipe does not make an authentic cubano, but that's okay—I never saw a Cuban sandwich when I traveled around Cuba! I did encounter quite a few mojitos, though. That mint, lime, and rum cocktail inspired one of the mayonnaises that flavor this sandwich. I usually make these sandwiches after the holidays with leftover turkey, but deli turkey is good too. Emmenthaler cheese from Switzerland is what our domestic Swiss cheese imitates. Use it or good quality Swiss. Putting a heavy weight on the sandwiches while grilling pushes the melted cheese into the bread and the bread onto the grill, making the sandwich crispy and compact. If you have an electric panini machine, this would be the perfect time to use it.

YIELD: 6 SANDWICHES

Sriracha Mayonnaise
½ cup mayonnaise, preferably organic

1 tablespoon Sriracha sauce

Sandwiches
1 (20-inch-long) loaf ciabatta
   or 6 (3-inch) ciabatta rolls

12 deli slices Emmenthaler or Swiss cheese

6 slices Black Forest ham

6 slices roast or smoked turkey breast

4 tablespoons unsalted butter

Mojito Mayonnaise
½ cup mayonnaise, preferably organic

⅓ cup finely chopped fresh mint

2 tablespoons fresh lime juice

2 tablespoons minced shallot

1 teaspoon sugar

1 teaspoon ground cumin

To make the Sriracha mayonnaise: Mix the mayonnaise with the Sriracha sauce in a small bowl.

To make the mojito mayonnaise: Mix the mayonnaise, mint, lime juice, shallot, sugar, and cumin together in another small bowl.

To assemble the sandwiches: Cut the ends off the ciabatta and cut the loaf into 6 even pieces (about 3 inches wide). Split the pieces in half lengthwise. Spread the Sriracha mayonnaise on the insides of the bread. Top the bottom halves with one slice of cheese, one slice of ham, and one slice of turkey. Spoon some mojito mayonnaise over the turkey, dividing evenly. Place a cheese slice atop the mojito mayonnaise and top with the remaining bread halves.

Working in batches, melt 1 tablespoon of butter on a heavy, large flat griddle over medium heat. Add half the sandwiches and top with a piece of aluminum foil. Place a large flat metal pan or small baking sheet atop the sandwiches, being careful not to displace the sandwich fillings. Place a brick or a few pounds of canned goods on the pan and cook until the bread is golden brown, about 4 minutes. Remove the weight, foil, and sandwiches. (Alternatively, grill the sandwiches in a panini machine.)

Melt 1 tablespoon of the butter on the griddle. Turn the sandwiches and replace the foil, pan, and weight. Continue cooking until the sandwiches are golden brown on the second side, the cheese is melted, and the meat is heated through, about 4 minutes longer. Repeat with the remaining butter and sandwiches. Cut the sandwiches in half on the diagonal and serve.

Grilled Chipotle Chicken and Cheddar Sandwiches

All the alliteration in this sandwich's name makes it sound like a fast food or chain restaurant offering, but it really is tasty. Chipotle chiles are dried, smoked jalapeño chiles. The hot chile comes dried or stewed in cans in adobo sauce. Keep unused chiles in adobo in a small plastic container in the freezer. You can use a panini grill for this recipe, if you like. Serve it for lunch or dinner with the Mexican Fruit "Gazpacho" Salad on page 87.

YIELD: 4 SANDWICHES

2 small boneless, skinless chicken breasts

Salt and pepper

3 tablespoons extra-virgin olive oil

1 to 2 teaspoons chopped canned chipotle chiles in adobo

8 ounces sharp Cheddar cheese, thinly sliced

8 slices sourdough sandwich bread

¼ cup cilantro leaves

Cut the chicken into strips and season it with salt and pepper. Heat 1 tablespoon of the olive oil in a griddle or large skillet over medium-high heat. Add the chicken to the skillet and stir-fry until cooked through, about 5 minutes. Transfer the chicken to a plate and cool slightly. Toss the chicken and the chipotle chiles together.

Arrange half the cheese on 4 slices of bread. Divide the chicken evenly among the bread slices and sprinkle the cilantro over the chicken. Top with the remaining cheese and bread.

Heat the remaining 2 tablespoons olive oil on the same griddle over medium heat. Add the sandwiches and cook until they are golden brown on both sides and the cheese melts, turning once, about 8 minutes. Transfer the sandwiches to a cutting board, cut in half, and serve.

Grilled Raclette Sandwiches with Shallots and Sage

Raclette cheese is a nutty cow's milk cheese made in Switzerland and France. Traditionally, cowherders would place a large round of raclette by an open fire and, as the cheese warmed to the right consistency, they scraped the outermost melted layer onto pieces of country bread, boiled potatoes, and sausages. Today you can buy little electric tabletop grills that melt the cheese gently—they're kind of silly, but the cheese does melt beautifully. It's creamy and stretchy, so it makes excellent grilled sandwiches.

YIELD: 2 SANDWICHES

2½ tablespoons butter, at room temperature

1 large shallot, thinly sliced

4 ounces raclette cheese, trimmed and sliced

4 slices (about 3 by 6 inches each) crusty sourdough bread

4 fresh sage leaves, thinly sliced

Pepper

Melt ½ tablespoon of the butter on a griddle or in a frying pan over medium heat. Add the shallot and cook without stirring, turning once, until it is golden brown and tender, about 3 minutes. Transfer the shallot to a small plate.

Arrange the cheese evenly over 2 slices of the bread. Sprinkle the shallot and sage over the cheese, distributing evenly, and season with pepper to taste. Top with the remaining bread slices.

Melt 1 tablespoon of the butter on the same griddle or frying pan. Add the sandwiches and spread the top slices of bread with the remaining 1 tablespoon butter. Cook until browned, about 2 minutes. Turn the sandwiches and cook until the second sides are browned, about 2 minutes longer.

Pizza Dough

White whole wheat flour, available at most markets and health food stores, is milder than traditional whole wheat flour milled from red wheat—it adds a nice flavor to the pizza crust. If you are unable to find it, you can add additional unbleached flour instead. The addition of wheat gluten flour makes a wonderful, slightly chewy crust. When I make pizza dough, I usually make a large batch, as the dough will keep in the refrigerator for a couple of days and it can be frozen for up to a month. I've included the amounts for a single pizza too.

YIELD: THREE 8-OUNCE BALLS PIZZA DOUGH

1 cup lukewarm water

1½ teaspoons active dry yeast

2¼ cups unbleached all-purpose flour

½ cup white whole wheat flour

3 tablespoons vital wheat gluten flour

1½ teaspoons kosher salt

¼ cup extra-virgin olive oil

Whisk the water and yeast together in a 2-cup measuring cup and let stand for 5 minutes.

Combine the flours and salt in a food processor and pulse to blend. Whisk the olive oil into the yeast mixture. With the food processor running, pour the yeast mixture through the feed tube and process until the dough forms a ball, about 1 minute. (If the dough does not form a ball, add lukewarm water by teaspoons until the dough comes together.)

Knead the dough briefly on a lightly floured surface for about 1 minute. Brush a large bowl with olive oil. Transfer the dough to the bowl and turn the dough to coat it with oil. Cover the bowl with a clean towel and let the dough stand until it doubles in volume, about 1½ hours.

Punch the dough down. Divide the dough into 3 even balls, about 8-ounces each. (*Can be made ahead. Place balls individually in resealable bags and refrigerate up to 2 days or freeze for 1 month. Let the refrigerated dough stand for 1 hour and frozen dough thaw 4 hours at room temperature before rolling.*)

For 1 pizza:

⅓ cup lukewarm water

½ teaspoon active dry yeast

¾ cup unbleached all-purpose flour

3 tablespoons white whole wheat flour

1 tablespoon vital wheat gluten flour

½ teaspoon kosher salt

1 tablespoon extra-virgin olive oil

Follow the directions in the main recipe, but reduce the rising time to about 1 hour.

Note: *Vital wheat gluten flour is sold by Bob's Red Mill.*

Sausage and Fennel Pizza

Sweet Italian sausage is raw pork sausage seasoned with fennel seeds. When you add sautéed fresh fennel and additional fennel seeds, this pizza bursts with sweet licorice-like flavor.

YIELD: ONE 12-INCH PIZZA

8 ounces Pizza Dough (page 120)
1 large fennel bulb, halved and thinly sliced, including fronds
3 links sweet Italian sausage (about 12 ounces), casings removed
½ teaspoon fennel seeds
2 garlic cloves, chopped
Cornmeal
1½ cups (6 ounces) grated mozzarella cheese
⅓ cup freshly grated Parmesan cheese
Salt and pepper

Prepare the pizza dough as directed in the recipe.

Heat a heavy, medium-sized skillet over medium heat. Add the sausage and cook, breaking into pieces with a wooden spoon, until browned and cooked through, about 8 minutes. Using a slotted spoon, transfer the sausage to a bowl. Drain all but 1 tablespoon of fat from the skillet. Sprinkle the fennel seeds into the skillet and stir until they are golden and fragrant, about 2 minutes.

Add the fennel slices and garlic to the skillet and sauté until the fennel is golden brown and almost tender, about 12 minutes. Transfer the mixture to the bowl with the sausage. *(The sausage and fennel can be prepared up to 1 day ahead. Cover and refrigerate.)*

Position one rack in the top and one rack in the bottom third of the oven and preheat it to 400°F. Sprinkle a heavy, large baking sheet lightly with cornmeal (about 1 tablespoon).

Roll the pizza dough out on a lightly floured surface to a 12-inch round. Transfer the dough to the prepared baking sheet and sprinkle evenly with mozzarella. Scatter the fennel and sausage mixture over the cheese. Sprinkle Parmesan cheese over the top and season lightly with salt and pepper. Bake until the pizza is golden brown on the bottom, about 15 minutes.

Transfer the pizza to the top rack and bake until golden, about 3 minutes. Transfer to a cutting board and sprinkle with the reserved fennel fronds. Cut into wedges and serve.

Brie and Prosciutto Pizza with Arugula

Even though I could easily eat this whole pizza myself—I love the sweet creaminess of the cheese with the salty Italian ham and tart, lemony greens—I often share this unusual pizza with friends as an appetizer.

YIELD: ONE 12-INCH PIZZA

8 ounces Pizza Dough (page 120)
8 ounces double-cream Brie
Cornmeal
3 to 4 thin slices prosciutto
2 cups arugula leaves
1 tablespoon fresh lemon juice
2 teaspoons extra-virgin olive oil
1 garlic clove, pressed
Pepper

Prepare the pizza dough as directed in the recipe.

Place the Brie in the freezer until it is firm but not solid, about 15 minutes. Trim off the rind and cut the Brie into ¼-inch-thick slices. Arrange the slices on a waxed-paper-lined pan and refrigerate.

Position one rack in the bottom third of the oven and preheat it to 400°F. Sprinkle a heavy, large baking sheet lightly with cornmeal (about 1 tablespoon).

Roll the pizza dough out on a lightly floured surface to a 12-inch round. Transfer the dough to the prepared sheet. Distribute the Brie evenly on top of the dough. Bake the pizza until the Brie melts and the crust is golden brown on the bottom, about 15 minutes. Transfer the pizza to a cutting board. Distribute the prosciutto evenly on top of the pizza.

Toss the arugula with the lemon juice, olive oil, and garlic in a medium-sized bowl. Top the pizza with the arugula and season with pepper. Cut into wedges and serve.

Radicchio, Red Onions, and Gorgonzola Pizza

Radicchio is a bitter, purple-leafed vegetable from the chicory family. It's great in a salad, but it's also tasty when slightly wilted and paired with the rich Italian blue cheese on top of this pizza.

YIELD: ONE 12-INCH PIZZA

8 ounces Pizza Dough (page 120)

1 tablespoon extra-virgin olive oil, plus more for brushing

1 red onion, sliced

Cornmeal

1 garlic clove, pressed

1 cup grated mozzarella cheese

1 cup finely sliced radicchio, lightly packed

2 ounces Gorgonzola cheese, crumbled

Salt

¼ teaspoon finely crumbled crushed red pepper flakes

2 tablespoons chopped fresh flat-leaf parsley, optional

Prepare the pizza dough as directed in the recipe.

Heat the olive oil in a medium-sized skillet over medium heat. Add the onion and sauté until tender, about 8 minutes. (Can be prepared to this point up to 1 day ahead. Transfer to an airtight container and refrigerate.)

Position one rack in the top and one rack in the bottom third of the oven and pre-heat it to 400°F. Sprinkle a heavy, large baking sheet lightly with cornmeal (about 1 tablespoon).

Roll the dough out on a lightly floured surface to a 12-inch round. Transfer the dough to the prepared baking sheet and brush with oil. Using your fingertips or the back of a spoon, spread the garlic over the dough. Sprinkle evenly with mozzarella. Distribute the onions and radicchio evenly over the top. Sprinkle with Gorgonzola. Season with salt and crushed red pepper flakes. Bake on the bottom rack until the bottom of the pizza is golden brown, about 15 minutes. Transfer the pizza to the top rack and bake until the top is golden, about 3 minutes. Transfer the pizza to a cutting board and sprinkle with parsley. Cut into wedges and serve.

Wild Mushroom Pizza with Fontina and Chives

This is sort of a fancy pizza—it's really tasty served with Champagne or Prosecco as a first course. Italian Fontina is softer and nuttier in flavor than the domestic variety. Look for it at specialty food stores, Italian markets, and cheese shops.

YIELD: ONE 12-INCH PIZZA

8 ounces Pizza Dough (page 120)
1 tablespoon extra-virgin olive oil, plus more for brushing
6 ounces assorted wild mushrooms (such as shiitake, chanterelle, or oyster), sliced
Salt
Cornmeal
1½ cups (about 6 ounces) grated Italian Fontina cheese
¼ cup freshly grated Parmesan cheese
2 tablespoons chopped fresh chives

Prepare the pizza dough as directed in the recipe.

Heat the olive oil in a heavy, large skillet over medium-high heat. Add the mushrooms and sauté until tender, about 5 minutes. Season the mushrooms with salt. *(Can be prepared to this point up to 2 days ahead. Transfer to a small container and refrigerate.)*

Position one rack in the top and one rack in the bottom third of the oven and preheat it to 400°F. Sprinkle a heavy, large baking sheet lightly with cornmeal (about 1 tablespoon).

Roll the dough out on a lightly floured surface to a 12-inch round. Transfer the dough to the prepared baking sheet and brush with oil. Sprinkle the Fontina cheese evenly over the dough. Distribute the mushrooms evenly over the cheese. Sprinkle the Parmesan cheese over the mushrooms. Bake the pizza on the bottom rack until the crust is golden brown on the bottom, about 15 minutes. Transfer the pizza to the top rack and bake until the top is golden brown, about 3 minutes. Transfer the pizza to a cutting board and sprinkle with the chives. Cut into wedges and serve.

Cherry Tomato, Goat Cheese, and Fresh Basil Pizza

This is a take on the classic Pizza Margherita—tomato, mozzarella, and basil pizza. I use cherry tomatoes and add a crumble of fresh goat cheese. You can use two thinly sliced tomatoes in place of the cherry tomatoes—just be sure to drain any excess moisture from the tomatoes to keep the pizza from getting soggy. Goat cheese crumbles easily when it's well chilled.

YIELD: ONE 12-INCH PIZZA

8 ounces Pizza Dough (page 120)
Cornmeal
Extra-virgin olive oil
1 garlic clove, pressed
1½ cups (about 6 ounces) grated mozzarella cheese
1 cup very small cherry tomatoes, cut in half
Salt and pepper
3 ounces goat cheese, crumbled
¼ cup chopped fresh basil

Prepare the pizza dough as directed in the recipe.

Position one rack in the top and one rack in the bottom third of the oven and preheat it to 400°F. Sprinkle a heavy, large baking sheet lightly with cornmeal (about 1 tablespoon).

Roll the dough out on a lightly floured surface to a 12-inch round. Transfer the dough to the prepared baking sheet and brush with oil. Using your fingertips or the back of a spoon, spread the garlic over the dough. Sprinkle evenly with the mozzarella and top with the tomatoes. Season the pizza lightly with salt and pepper and sprinkle with the goat cheese. Bake on the bottom rack until the bottom of the pizza is golden brown, about 15 minutes. Transfer the pizza to the top rack and bake until the top is golden, about 3 minutes. Transfer the pizza to a cutting board and sprinkle with basil. Cut into wedges and serve.

Tarte Flambé
(Alsatian Bacon and Onion Pizza)

Called a "fired tart" because it's traditionally cooked in a wood-fired oven, *tarte flambé* or *flammekueche* is the pizza of Alsace. Topped with onions and bacon, my favorite version is made with Gruyère cheese. Serve it as an appetizer or for dinner, but always pour a nice glass of Riesling for a blissful combo.

YIELD: ONE 11-INCH SQUARE PIZZA

8 ounces Pizza Dough (page 120)

4 ounces thickly sliced applewood-smoked bacon (about 3 slices)

2 onions, sliced

⅓ cup white wine

1 tablespoon fresh thyme leaves

Salt and pepper

Cornmeal

¼ cup sour cream

2 cups (about 8 ounces) grated Gruyère cheese

Prepare the pizza dough as directed in the recipe.

Cut the bacon into $\frac{1}{2}$-inch pieces and cook them in a heavy, large skillet over medium heat until just crisp, about 8 minutes. Using a slotted spoon, transfer the bacon to a paper-towel-lined plate. Drain off all but 1 tablespoon of the bacon fat from the skillet. Add the onions to the skillet and sauté over medium heat until golden brown and tender, about 25 minutes.

Add the wine and half of the thyme leaves to the skillet and cook until the wine is absorbed and the onions are very tender, about 4 minutes. Season the onions with salt and pepper to taste. *(Can be prepared to this point up to 2 days ahead; cover the onions and bacon separately and refrigerate.)*

Position a rack in the bottom third of the oven and preheat it to 400°F. Sprinkle a heavy, large baking sheet lightly with cornmeal (about 1 tablespoon).

Roll the dough out on a lightly floured surface to an 11-inch square. Transfer the dough to the prepared baking sheet. Leaving a $\frac{1}{2}$-inch border, spread the sour cream evenly over the dough. Sprinkle the cheese evenly over the sour cream. Distribute the onions over the cheese and sprinkle the bacon over the onions. Bake until the crust is golden brown on the bottom, about 15 minutes.

Slide the pizza onto a cutting board, sprinkle with the remaining thyme, and cool slightly. Cut into pieces and serve.

Seeded Flat Bread Pizza with Olives, Feta, and Harissa Drizzle

Feta cheese, fresh mint, and cumin seeds are not your basic pizza toppings, but this Mediter-ranean-influenced pizza is not your basic pizza. Enjoy it as an appetizer or a light main course when paired with the Eggplant and Herb Salad with Lemony Sumac Dressing (page 84). Harissa is a spicy condiment from North Africa made from red peppers and spices. You can purchase harissa in jars, tubes, and cans, but the heat varies greatly. This drizzle, a mild version of the sauce, is good on grilled fish or used as a dipping sauce for pita chips.

YIELD: ONE 12-INCH PIZZA

8 ounces Pizza Dough (page 120)

Harissa Drizzle

1 large red bell pepper or 1 (7.4-ounce) jar
   roasted red bell peppers, drained
½ teaspoon cumin seeds
½ teaspoon caraway seeds
2 tablespoons extra-virgin olive oil
1 tablespoon fresh lemon juice
2 garlic cloves
1 to 2 teaspoons sambal oelek
Salt and pepper

Pizza

½ teaspoon fennel seeds
½ teaspoon cumin seeds
Extra-virgin olive oil
1 cup crumbled feta cheese
½ cup pitted green olives, sliced
2 green onions, finely chopped
2 tablespoon chopped fresh mint
1 tablespoon chopped fresh flat-leaf parsley

Prepare the pizza dough as directed in the recipe.

To make the drizzle: Char the bell pepper over a gas flame or under the broiler until blackened and charred on all sides. Transfer to a bowl and cover with plastic, allowing the pepper to steam while cooling. Peel, seed, and stem the pepper.

Toast the cumin and caraway seeds in a heavy, small skillet over medium-high heat, stirring until they are golden brown and fragrant, about 2 minutes. Transfer the seeds to the blender. Add the pepper, olive oil, lemon juice, and garlic and purée until smooth. Add the sambal oelek to taste. Season with salt and pepper. *(Can be prepared up to 1 week ahead. Transfer to an airtight jar and keep refrigerated.)*

To make the pizza: Generously oil the grill and set it to medium-low heat.

Roll the dough out on a lightly floured surface to a 10-inch round. Sprinkle the fennel and cumin seeds over the surface of the dough and roll it out to a 12-inch round, pressing the seeds into the dough while rolling. Transfer the dough to a large baking sheet. Brush the top of the dough generously with olive oil. Place the dough on the grill, oiled side down. Brush the top of the dough with oil and grill until the bottom side is golden brown, about 3 minutes. Carefully rotate the dough to prevent burning. Using tongs, carefully turn the dough over. Immediately sprinkle the feta cheese and olives on the dough. Grill until the bottom of the pizza is golden brown, about 3 minutes, rotating the pizza to prevent burning.

Transfer the pizza to a cutting board and spoon the Harissa Drizzle evenly over the pizza. Sprinkle with green onions, mint, and parsley. Cut into wedges and serve.

Feta cheese is made from goat, sheep, or cow milk. The curds are salted and cured in a brine of water or whey. Some people don't like the strong and salty cheese, but not all feta cheese is the same. French feta, made from sheep's milk cheese, is mild and creamy; I like to cook with it as it is not too salty. Bulgarian feta is very good too, and the feta that I ate in Turkey was the best I've ever tasted.

Grilled Gorgonzola and Pine Nut Pizza

I like to make pizza on the grill on summer evenings when it's too hot to turn on the oven. For parties, I'll make three pizzas and serve them cut into small wedges as an appetizer before I put something else on the grill. When paired with a salad, it makes for a good summer supper.

YIELD: ONE 12-INCH PIZZA (RECIPE TRIPLES EASILY)

8 ounces Pizza Dough (page 120)

2 tablespoons extra-virgin olive oil

1 garlic clove, pressed

1 cup shredded mozzarella cheese

3 ounces Gorgonzola cheese, crumbled

3 tablespoons pine nuts

2 tablespoons chopped fresh basil

Prepare the pizza dough as directed in the recipe.

Generously oil the grill (see sidebar) and set it to medium-low heat.

Combine the oil and the garlic in a small bowl. Roll the dough out on a lightly floured surface to a 12-inch round. Transfer the dough to a large baking sheet. Brush the top of the dough generously with the garlic oil. Place the dough on the grill, oiled side down. Brush the top of the dough with the garlic oil and grill until the bottom side is golden brown, about 3 minutes, carefully rotating the dough to prevent burning. Using tongs, carefully turn the dough over. Immediately sprinkle the mozzarella, Gorgonzola, and pine nuts over the dough. Grill until the bottom of the pizza is golden brown and the cheeses melt, about 3 minutes. Rotate the pizza to prevent burning.

Transfer the pizza to a cutting board and sprinkle with basil. Cut into wedges and serve.

Pizza on the Barbie

Pizza made on the grill is delicious and, with a little practice, fun and easy to make. Grilled pizzas don't have a lot of toppings on them since the dough browns too quickly to cook a thick layer of goodies. Keep toppings simple and flavorful, like strong cheeses and/or lots of herbs and spices.

Start with a well-seasoned grill. Using newspaper or paper towels, rub vegetable shortening on the grill or spray with non-stick grill spray before lighting. Place the rolled-out pizza dough on a lightly floured, wax-paper-lined baking sheet and keep covered until ready to use. Make sure all your toppings are handy before you put the pizza dough on the grill. Sprinkle the cheese on the cooked side of the dough as soon as you turn it over—you will need the residual heat to melt the cheese. If for some reason the cheese does not melt adequately before the bottom crust gets too brown, broil the pizza briefly before serving.

While it's easier to control the heat on a gas grill, I've made pizzas on my charcoal barbecue with success too. When grilling over charcoal, make sure the coals have burned down sufficiently.

Penne with Asparagus, Fresh Ricotta, and Green Garlic

This elegant "pasta toss" showcases the best of spring, with baby asparagus, green garlic, a hint of lemon, and fresh ricotta. Ricotta is made from whey, meaning it's actually a by-product of another cheese, such as mozzarella. Look for whole-milk ricotta that's labeled "fresh" for the best quality—you'll find it at Italian and specialty food markets. Use fresh ricotta soon after purchase, as it spoils quickly.

YIELD: 4 TO 6 SERVINGS

15 ounces fresh ricotta cheese

½ cup freshly grated Parmesan cheese, plus more for serving

3 tablespoons minced green garlic or 2 large garlic cloves, crushed

1 teaspoon grated lemon zest

Salt and pepper

1 pound penne pasta

1 pound thin asparagus, cut diagonally into 2-inch pieces

Mix the ricotta, Parmesan, garlic, and lemon zest together in a large serving bowl. Season with salt and pepper to taste.

Boil the pasta in a large pot of rapidly boiling, generously salted water until almost tender, but still firm to bite, 8 to 10 minutes.

Add the asparagus to the pasta and boil until the asparagus is just crisp-tender, 2 to 3 minutes. Drain the pasta and asparagus, reserving ½ cup of the cooking water. Immediately add the pasta and asparagus to the cheese mixture along with the reserved cooking water. Toss to coat thoroughly. Taste to adjust seasoning and serve with additional Parmesan.

Cooking Pasta

To successfully cook pasta, start by bringing a large pot of water to boil. There should be enough water in the pot so each piece of pasta can float freely, about 4 quarts of water per pound of pasta. Once the water boils rapidly, add a generous amount of kosher salt, about 1½ tablespoons. This may seem like a lot, but inadequately salted water will effectively leach pasta of its flavor. Add the pasta to the rapidly boiling water and stir it with a wooden spoon to keep it from clumping and sticking. Maintain a steady boil and stir the pasta occasionally.

To check the pasta for doneness, remove a piece from the water with tongs and cool it slightly. Taste the pasta: it should be flexible and tender, but still slightly firm to bite. The cooking time can vary from a few minutes up to about 15 minutes, depending on the shape and size of the pasta. When the pasta is cooked, remove it from the heat and reserve any needed pasta cooking water with a heat-proof measuring cup or ladle. Drain the pasta with a colander. I like to place a pasta serving bowl in the sink and set a colander above it. Draining the hot water into the serving bowl and allowing it to sit for a minute or two before carefully emptying it, warms the bowl so that it keeps the pasta hot at the table. Mix the cooked pasta with sauce.

Never rinse pasta. Rinsing pasta strips it of taste and somehow makes it less able to absorb the flavors of the sauce.

Orecchiette with Tomatoes and Garden Herbs

I like to make this simple pasta with the pretty, sweet, yellow sungold cherry tomatoes that grow in a pot on my patio. The "little ears" (*orecchiette*) cup the tomatoes neatly. I use a handful of herbs from the garden—usually a mixture of basil, oregano, and chives—to add fresh flavor, but flat-leaf parsley and arugula work well too. If you've got a surplus of larger tomatoes, dice enough to measure 3½ cups to toss with the pasta. Be sure to use the best quality extra-virgin olive oil when preparing this dish.

YIELD: 4 TO 6 SERVINGS

8 ounces orecchiette (ear-shaped pasta)

1 pound yellow, red, and/or orange cherry
   or grape tomatoes, cut in half (about 3½ cups)

3 tablespoons extra-virgin olive oil

2 tablespoons white balsamic vinegar

2 garlic cloves, pressed

Salt and pepper

⅔ cup chopped fresh herbs (such as basil, oregano, and chives)

½ cup coarsely grated Parmesan or Pecorino Romano cheese

Cook the pasta in a large pot of boiling salted water until it is tender but still firm to bite, stirring occasionally, about 10 minutes. Drain.

Meanwhile, combine the tomatoes, oil, vinegar, and garlic in a large bowl. Add the pasta and season with salt and pepper to taste. Stir in the herbs and cheese, and serve warm or at room temperature.

Sugo di Carne with Rigatoni

Sugo di Carne simply means "meat sauce," and fortunately, preparing this rich, meaty, home-style pasta is equally simple. This serves a crowd with ease. You can make the sauce ahead, so it's a great dish for entertaining. Start the meal with an antipasti of olives, sliced fennel, and Parmesan, serve a radicchio and spinach salad along with the pasta, and finish the meal with amaretti cookies and gelati.

YIELD: 12 SERVINGS

3 to 4 tablespoons olive oil

3½ pounds boneless chuck, trimmed and cut into 2-inch pieces

Salt and pepper

2 very large onions, sliced

3 (14-ounce) cans diced tomatoes with basil, garlic, and oregano

1 (750-ml) bottle Chianti

1 cup espresso or very strong coffee

10 garlic cloves, chopped

4 large sprigs fresh oregano or 1 generous teaspoon dried

½ teaspoon crushed red pepper flakes

2 pounds rigatoni pasta

½ cup finely chopped flat-leaf parsley

Preheat the oven to 350°F.

Heat 3 tablespoons of the olive oil in a heavy, large Dutch oven over medium-high heat. Season the meat with salt and pepper. Add the meat to the Dutch oven in batches and cook until browned, about 4 minutes per batch. Transfer the meat to a large bowl. Add the onions and the remaining 1 tablespoon of olive oil to the Dutch oven and sauté until tender, about 5 minutes. Return the meat to the Dutch oven. Add the tomatoes, wine, espresso, garlic, oregano, and red pepper flakes and bring to a simmer. Cover and cook in the oven until the meat is very tender and beginning to fall apart, about 2½ hours.

Let the meat cool slightly then season with salt and pepper to taste. *(Or cool and refrigerate overnight. Can be made to this point up to 3 days ahead. Reheat in a 350°F. oven or over low heat, stirring frequently until heated through.)*

Meanwhile, boil the pasta in large pot of generously salted water until tender but firm to bite, about 14 minutes. Drain well.

Using two forks, coarsely shred the meat. Toss the pasta and the meat sauce together in a very large bowl. Sprinkle with parsley and serve.

Fettuccine with Shiitake Mushrooms, Cavalo Nero, and Rosemary

Cavalo nero (black kale) is a dark green hearty member of the cabbage family that is also called dinosaur, Tuscan, or lacinato kale. It's delicious with the rich mushrooms and cream in this pasta dish.

YIELD: 6 SERVINGS

1 tablespoon extra-virgin olive oil
1 large onion, finely chopped
6 ounces shiitake mushrooms, stemmed and sliced
6 garlic cloves, finely chopped
1 bunch *cavalo nero* or Tuscan kale, cut crosswise into ¼-inch slices
2 teaspoons finely chopped fresh rosemary
½ teaspoon crushed red pepper flakes
Salt
1 pound fettuccine
½ cup heavy cream
1 cup freshly grated Parmesan cheese

Heat the olive oil in a heavy, very large skillet over medium heat. Add the onion and sauté until tender, about 5 minutes. Add the mushrooms and sauté until tender and golden, about 6 minutes. Stir in the garlic and cook for 2 minutes. Add the *cavalo nero* and cook, stirring occasionally, until it wilts, about 5 minutes. Stir in the rosemary and red pepper flakes, and season with salt to taste.

Meanwhile, cook the pasta in a large pot of generously salted rapidly boiling water until it is tender but still firm to bite, about 10 minutes. Drain, reserving 1½ cups of the pasta cooking water. Add 1 cup of the pasta cooking water to the mushroom mixture in the skillet. Simmer until the *cavalo nero* is tender and the liquid in the skillet is reduced by half, about 3 minutes. Stir in the cream. Add the pasta to the mushroom mixture cheese along with half the Parmesan cheese, and toss to combine. Add a small amount of additional reserved pasta cooking water if necessary to moisten the pasta. Serve, passing the remaining Parmesan separately.

Linguine Carbonara with Zucchini

My daughters have always loved the Roman bacon and egg pasta named for the charcoal maker's wife. I started sneaking zucchini into it one evening in late summer when faced with a bumper crop of the squash—you can leave it out and use pancetta instead of bacon if you're a purist.

YIELD: 4 SERVINGS

4 ounces applewood-smoked bacon
½ onion, thinly sliced
3 medium zucchini, sliced into ¼-inch thick rounds
½ pound linguine
2 eggs, at room temperature
½ cup freshly grated Parmesan cheese, plus more for serving
Salt and pepper
2 tablespoons chopped fresh flat-leaf parsley, optional

Cut the bacon crosswise into ½-inch pieces and fry in a heavy, large skillet over medium heat until crisp. Using a slotted spoon, transfer the bacon to a paper towel to drain. Pour off all but 2 tablespoons of the fat from the skillet and save for another use. Add the onion to the skillet and sauté over medium-high heat until just golden brown, about 6 minutes. Add the zucchini and sauté until it is golden brown and just tender, about 4 minutes.

Meanwhile, cook the pasta in a large pot of rapidly boiling, generously salted water until tender but still firm to bite, about 9 minutes. Drain the pasta, reserving ½ cup of the cooking water. Whisk the eggs together in a medium-sized bowl, then add the Parmesan cheese, a generous pinch of salt, and a grinding of pepper. Gradually whisk in ¼ cup of the cooking water.

Add the pasta to the zucchini mixture in the skillet and heat briefly. Remove the skillet from the heat. Pour the egg mixture into the pasta and stir until the pasta is creamy—not wet with runny raw egg or dry with curdled eggs—about 2 minutes (return the skillet to very low heat if necessary). Add some of the remaining cooking water if necessary to moisten. Stir in the bacon and parsley.

Serve the pasta in shallow bowls, passing the additional Parmesan cheese separately.

Baked Ziti and Cauliflower with Cheese

This is like a cross between macaroni and cheese and a cauliflower gratin—two of my favorite comfort foods. It really is best the day it's made, but it's still delicious if made ahead.

YIELD: 8 TO 10 SERVINGS

4 tablespoons unsalted butter

1 cup chopped onion

2 garlic cloves, minced

⅓ cup unbleached all-purpose flour

3 cups cold milk

1 fresh or dried bay leaf

8 ounces Gruyère cheese, grated

8 ounces sharp white Cheddar cheese, grated

½ teaspoon salt

¼ teaspoon cayenne pepper

⅛ teaspoon freshly grated nutmeg

Pepper

¾ pound ziti pasta

1 head cauliflower, cut into florets, florets sliced

2 tablespoons chopped flat-leaf parsley, optional

1 cup panko (Japanese bread crumbs)

¼ cup freshly grated Parmesan cheese

Salt

Preheat the oven to 350°F. Butter a 13 x 9-inch baking dish.

Melt 2 tablespoons of the butter in a heavy, large pot over medium heat. Add the onion and sauté until translucent, about 5 minutes. Stir in the garlic, then the flour, and continue stirring 1 minute (do not brown the flour). Add the milk all at once along with the bay leaf. Cook, whisking occasionally, until the mixture just boils and thickens, about 8 minutes. Add the cheeses and simmer and stir until they melt. Stir in the salt, cayenne, pepper, and nutmeg. Remove the bay leaf and season the sauce with pepper. *(Can be prepared to this point up to 1 day ahead. Cool, cover, and refrigerate.)*

Meanwhile, cook the pasta in a large pot of rapidly boiling salted water until almost tender, about 8 minutes. Add the cauliflower to the pasta and continue boiling until the pasta and cauliflower are tender, about 4 minutes. Drain very well. Add the pasta and cauliflower to the cheese mixture and stir well. Mix in the parsley.

Transfer the pasta mixture to the prepared baking dish and smooth the top. Melt the remaining 2 tablespoons butter and combine with the panko in a small bowl. Add the Parmesan cheese and mix well. Season with salt and sprinkle evenly over the pasta. *(Can be prepared to this point up to 1 day ahead. Cover and refrigerate.)*

Bake until the crumbs are golden brown and the pasta bubbles at the edges and is heated through, about 30 minutes.

Sesame Noodles

These are the perfect noodles to eat out of a big bowl while in pajamas on a comfy couch watching a movie. But that doesn't mean they wouldn't be good served at a table with some stir-fried broccoli.

YIELD: 4 TO 6 SERVINGS

3 tablespoons tahini

3 tablespoons soy sauce

2 tablespoons light brown sugar, packed

1 teaspoon sambal oelek

8 green onions

6 garlic cloves

1½-inch piece fresh ginger, peeled

¾ pound spaghetti

3 tablespoons toasted sesame oil

1 red bell pepper, thinly sliced

Sambal Oelek is to Indonesian and Malaysian cuisine what salsa is to Mexican food. Just as there are countless variations of salsa, there are many styles and flavors of sambal. Sambal oelek, is the simplest, usually containing just red chile and salt. I like the clean heat it adds.

Whisk the tahini, soy sauce, brown sugar, and sambal oelek together in a small bowl. Thinly slice the green parts of the green onions and set aside. Mince the remainder of the green onions along with the garlic and ginger.

Cook the pasta in a large pot of boiling salted water until tender but still firm to bite, about 8 minutes.

Meanwhile, heat the sesame oil in a heavy, large skillet over medium-high heat. Add the bell pepper and stir-fry until almost tender, about 1 minute. Add the onion-garlic mixture and stir-fry until the onions and garlic are tender and begin to turn golden brown, about 1 minute.

Drain the noodles, reserving about ⅔ cup of the cooking water. Whisk half the reserved cooking water into the tahini mixture. Add the pasta to the skillet along with the tahini mixture and the reserved green onions. Stir over low heat until the noodles are just lightly coated, about 2 minutes, adding additional cooking water if necessary to moisten.

Orzo with Butternut Squash and Sage Cream

Orzo is a rice-shaped pasta. I made this rich, comforting dish one October evening when I was supposed to make a butternut squash lasagna for our annual pumpkin carving supper, but ran out of time. I whipped up this recipe in about 30 minutes, and it's become a keeper.

YIELD: 6 TO 8 SERVINGS

½ small butternut squash (about 10 ounces)

¾ cup heavy cream

12 large fresh sage leaves, sliced crosswise

4 tablespoons unsalted butter

1 pound orzo pasta

3 garlic cloves, minced

2½ cups chicken broth

¾ teaspoon kosher salt

½ cup freshly grated Parmesan cheese, plus more for sprinkling

Salt and pepper

Peel and seed the squash and cut it into 1-inch pieces. Put the squash in the food processor and pulse to coarsely chop it into ¼- to ½-inch pieces. (*Can be prepared up to 1 day ahead. Cover and chill.*)

Simmer the cream and sage leaves in a heavy, medium-sized saucepan over medium heat until reduced to ½ cup, about 2 minutes. Remove from the heat, cover, and set aside.

Melt the butter in a heavy, large saucepan over medium heat. Add the orzo and sauté until golden, about 5 minutes. Add the squash and garlic and mix well. Add 3 cups water, the broth, and salt, and bring to a simmer. Cook uncovered until the liquid is almost completely absorbed but the mixture is still slightly loose, about 13 minutes.

Stir the Parmesan cheese into the orzo and season with salt and pepper. Spoon the orzo into shallow bowls and drizzle with about 1 tablespoon of the sage cream. Sprinkle with additional cheese and serve immediately.

Variation: You can make a rosemary cream by substituting 1½ teaspoons minced fresh rosemary for the sage.

Grilled Fish Tacos with Cilantro and Lime Coleslaw

Teenagers love fish tacos and it gives a mom great pleasure to see them mound healthy cabbage onto their tortillas. Don't worry if you are unable to keep the snapper fillets whole while grilling—the fish gets broken into pieces anyway. If you don't want to barbecue, you can broil the fish instead.

YIELD: 4 TO 6 SERVINGS

Coleslaw

1 small head cabbage (about 1¼ pounds)

⅔ cup sour cream

3 tablespoons fresh lime juice

2 teaspoons ground cumin

1 garlic clove, pressed

½ teaspoon kosher salt

1 cup diced white onion

½ cup chopped cilantro

Fish

2 tablespoons extra-virgin olive oil

2 tablespoons minced or puréed
     canned chipotle chiles in adobo

1 tablespoon fresh lime juice

2 teaspoons ground cumin

1½ pounds red snapper fillets

Salt and pepper

12 corn tortillas

2 or 3 ripe avocados, peeled,
     pitted, and sliced

Picante sauce, such as Valentina

To make the coleslaw: Quarter, core, and thinly slice the cabbage (you should have about 6 cups). Stir the sour cream, lime juice, cumin, garlic, and salt together in a large bowl. Add the cabbage, onion, and cilantro, and stir together. Refrigerate. *(Can be prepared to this point up to 1 day ahead.)*

To prepare the fish: Mix the olive oil, chipotles, lime juice, and cumin in a 13 x 9-inch baking dish. Add the fish and turn to coat. *(Can be prepared to this point up to 8 hours ahead. Cover and refrigerate.)*

Preheat the grill to medium heat.

Place the fish fillets on the grill and season with salt and pepper. Grill the fish until just cooked through, about 3 minutes per side. Transfer the fish to a platter.

Meanwhile, heat the tortillas over an open gas flame or on a griddle. Wrap them in aluminum foil to keep warm.

Serve the fish, breaking it into large pieces with a serving spoon, with warm tortillas, avocados, coleslaw, and picante sauce, allowing your guests to assemble their own tacos.

Seared Halibut with Roasted Yellow Tomato and Green Olive Relish

Roasting brings out the sweetness of the tomatoes in this dish, and when mixed with green olives and fresh herbs, it's the perfect topping for tender halibut fillets. Of course you can use red grape or cherry tomatoes. There is just something so cool about the look of the yellow and green relish on the pretty, white fish.

YIELD: 4 SERVINGS

Relish

1 pound yellow grape or cherry tomatoes

2 tablespoons extra-virgin olive oil

2 garlic cloves, pressed

½ cup brine-cured green olives, chopped

2 green onions, sliced

2 tablespoons chopped fresh basil
  or tarragon

2 tablespoons fresh lemon juice

1 teaspoon grated lemon zest

Salt and pepper

Fish

1 tablespoon extra-virgin olive oil

4 (5- to 6-ounce) halibut fillets,
  about 1½-inches thick

Salt and pepper

⅓ cup dry white wine

Preheat the oven to 400°F.

To make the relish: Combine the tomatoes, olive oil, and garlic in a heavy, medium-sized roasting pan. Roast the tomatoes without stirring until lightly browned, about 10 minutes (the cooking time will depend on the size of the tomatoes). Remove from the oven and toss gently with the olives, green onions, basil, lemon juice, and lemon zest in a medium-sized bowl. Season with salt and pepper to taste. (*Can be made to this point several hours ahead; store covered at room temperature.*)

To prepare the fish: Heat the olive oil in a heavy, large skillet over medium-high heat. Add the halibut and season with salt and pepper. Cook until lightly browned, about 3 minutes. Turn the fillets and continue cooking until they are just cooked through, 2 to 3 minutes longer.

Transfer the halibut to individual plates. Spoon the relish over the halibut, dividing evenly. Add the wine to the skillet and stir over medium-high heat, scraping up the browned bits. Pour the pan juices over the halibut and relish, and serve.

Scallops with Three Peas and Prosciutto

The sweetness of peas brings out the sweetness of the scallops in this dish, while prosciutto rounds out the flavor. Although this dish requires a series of simple steps, all you'll need to complete the meal is a warm baguette. Pea sprouts are available at Whole Foods markets and other specialty food stores. You can also use young pea tendrils, *dau miu*, which are sold in Chinese markets and at some farmers' markets. If you can't find pea sprouts or tendrils, the dish is still great with only two types of peas! You can purchase bags of flash-frozen scallops at fish markets and at some Trader Joe's.

YIELD: 4 SERVINGS

8 ounces (1 cup) English peas, shelled, or frozen petit peas

8 ounces sugar snap peas or Chinese peas

3 tablespoons extra-virgin olive oil

1 large shallot, minced

¼ cup minced green garlic or 2 garlic cloves, minced

3 teaspoons minced fresh thyme

½ cup dry white wine

3 ounces (about 3 cups) pea sprouts

Salt and pepper

1¼ pounds jumbo wild-caught sea scallops

2 ounces thinly sliced prosciutto, chopped

Cook the English peas in a large pot of boiling salted water for 1 minute. Add the snap peas and boil until just tender, about 3 minutes. Drain. *(Can be prepared to this point up to 1 day ahead. Refrigerate in a small container.)*

Heat 1 tablespoon of the olive oil in a heavy, large skillet over medium heat. Add the shallot and cook until golden, about 3 minutes. Add the garlic and 2 teaspoons of the thyme and cook for 1 minute. Add the wine, then transfer the mixture to a measuring cup or small bowl.

Heat 1 tablespoon of the olive oil to the same skillet over medium-high heat. Add the peas and cook until heated through, about 3 minutes. Remove from the heat and immediately stir in the pea sprouts. Season with salt and pepper to taste. Transfer the mixture to a serving dish, cover with aluminum foil, and keep warm.

Heat the remaining 1 tablespoon olive oil in the same skillet over medium-high heat. Add the scallops and sprinkle the prosciutto around the scallops. Sprinkle the scallops with salt, pepper, and the remaining 1 teaspoon thyme. Cook until the scallops are browned on both sides, turning once and pushing the prosciutto to the edges of the skillet, about 3 minutes per side for the scallops. Using tongs, arrange the scallops atop the pea mixture in the serving dish; keep warm. Add the wine mixture to the prosciutto in the skillet and boil for 1 minute while stirring up the browned bits. Pour over the scallops and serve.

Clams with Chorizo and Saffron

Use smaller clams (about 1½ to 2 inches) for this recipe. I use Manila or little neck clams. If you can't find the firm, fully cooked Spanish chorizo, you can substitute pepperoni or a firm Italian sopressata. Serve with warm bread for sopping up the rich, mildly spicy broth and some salad greens on the side.

YIELD: 4 TO 6 SERVINGS

3 tablespoons extra-virgin olive oil

1 onion, chopped

3 ounces Spanish chorizo, diced

4 garlic cloves, sliced

⅛ teaspoon crushed saffron threads

1 cup clam juice

⅔ cup dry white wine

3 pounds small (about 1½ inches each) clams, rinsed

Chopped fresh flat-leaf parsley

Heat the olive oil in a heavy, large pot or deep skillet over medium heat. Add the onion and sauté until tender, about 8 minutes. Add the chorizo, garlic, and saffron and stir for 1 minute. Add the clam juice and wine and simmer until the mixture is reduced to 2 cups, about 4 minutes. Add the clams, cover, and cook until they open, about 5 minutes. (Discard any clams that do not open.)

Ladle the clams and broth into bowls, sprinkle with parsley, and serve.

Saffron gives food an intense golden yellow hue and a rich, slightly musky, old-world flavor. It has been used since the ancient Greeks. Saffron threads are the dried stigmas of the purple crocus sativus *flower. The spice is expensive because each crocus produces only three stigmas that must be carefully collected by hand. But a little of this Southwest Asian native goes along way. In fact, too much can result in a bitter flavor. You can actually grow saffron crocus in your garden—zones 6 to 8 in the south and 6 to 9 in the west. The corms are available from White Flower Farms (www.whiteflowerfarms.com).*

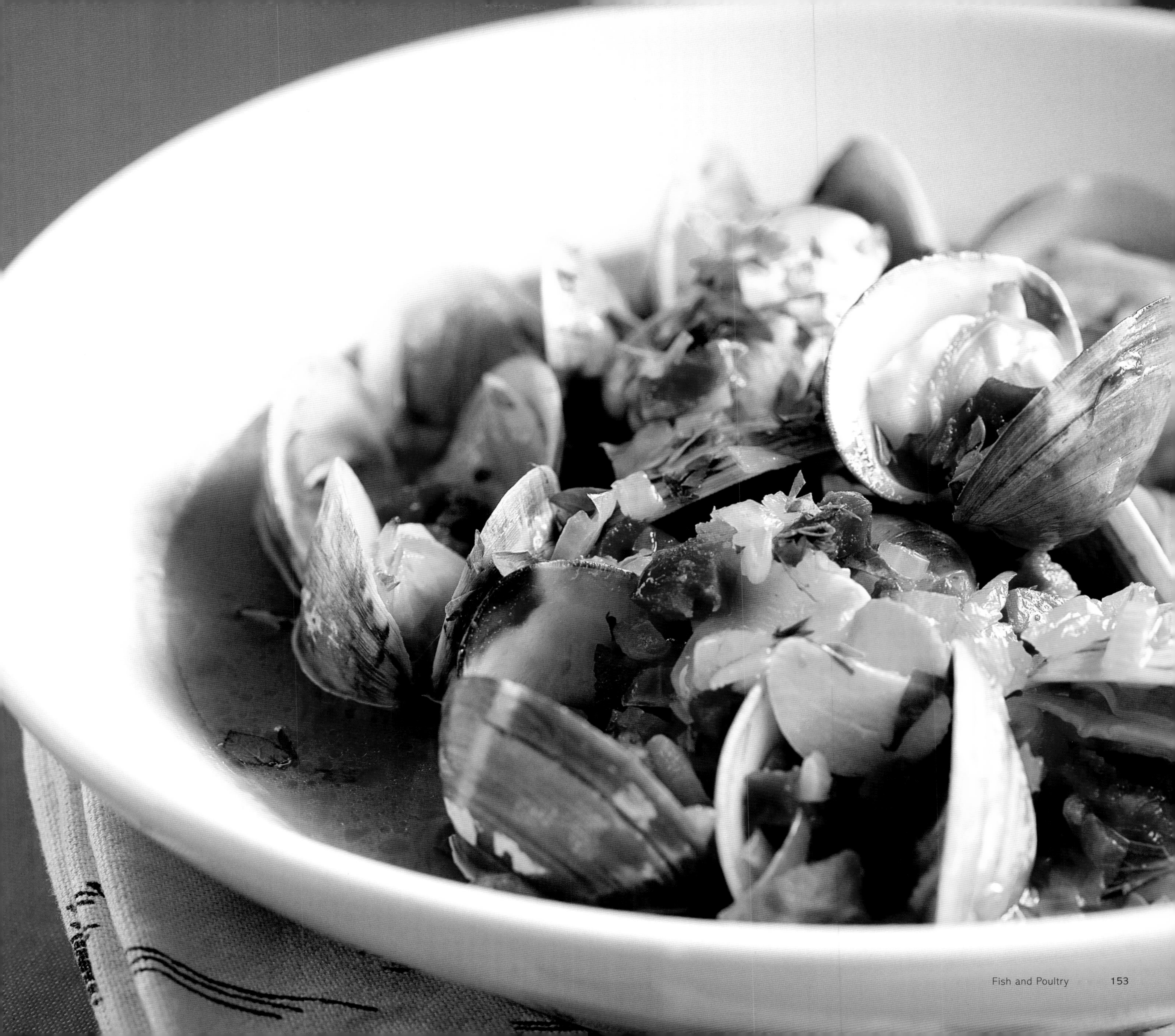

Albacore Kebabs with Charmoula

I have the good fortune to have a friend who gives me the most wonderful albacore, bluefin and ahi tuna, and yellowtail. Los Angeles artist Tim Ebner goes fishing a few times a year with his brother and enthusiastically shares his catch with his friends. After a day or two of enjoying the ultra-fresh fish raw, I like to make these kebabs. *Charmoula* is a North African condiment that mixes olive oil, herbs, spices, and garlic with lemon juice. Here it's used as a marinade and a tasty sauce. You can also use tuna or yellowtail for the kebabs.

YIELD: 4 SERVINGS; ABOUT 1 CUP *CHARMOULA*

Charmoula

1 tablespoon cumin seeds

1 cup coarsely chopped fresh cilantro

⅓ cup coarsely chopped flat-leaf parsley

2 garlic cloves

1 tablespoon fresh lemon juice

2 teaspoons paprika

⅓ cup extra-virgin olive oil

Salt and pepper

Kebabs

1 pound albacore, cut into 1½-inch cubes

12 cherry tomatoes

2 small zucchini (about 5 ounces each), cut into ½-inch thick rounds

Lemon wedges

To make the charmoula: Stir the cumin seeds in a small skillet over medium heat until lightly toasted and fragrant, about 2 minutes. Transfer the seeds to a food processor. Add the cilantro, parsley, garlic, lemon juice, and paprika, and pulse until everything is finely chopped and blended. With the processor running, pour in the olive oil. Process until the herbs are very finely minced. Transfer to a bowl and season with salt and pepper to taste. *(Can be made to this point up to 3 days ahead. Cover and refrigerate. Let stand at room temperature 1 hour before serving.)*

To prepare the kebabs: Thread the tuna onto metal or bamboo skewers (see note) alternating with the tomatoes and zucchini. Brush the kebabs with half the charmoula. Cover and refrigerate for at least 1 hour and up to 6 hours.

Prepare a grill to medium-high. Grill the kebabs until browned on all sides, turning occasionally, about 6 minutes. Transfer them to a platter and garnish with lemon wedges. Serve, passing the remaining charmoula separately.

Note: *Soak bamboo skewers in a large shallow baking dish with enough water to cover for at least 20 minutes before threading with fish. The water-logged skewers won't burn on the grill.*

Grilled Tuna Steaks with Shallot and Lime Leaf Sambal

I got to travel by boat to some very remote islands in Indonesia. My brother Matt, who lives in New Guinea, set up an amazing trip to the Banda islands for our entire family. At sea, we dined on freshly caught tuna steaks with a fresh *sambal*, or Indonesian-style salsa. This is my adaptation of what I saw the cook do. I think the simple, bright flavor really sets off the rich tuna perfectly. Serve this with steamed rice and the Asian Slaw with Spicy Peanut Dressing (page 88). Double or triple the recipe for a crowd. Use good-quality peanut oil, preferably roasted, available at specialty food stores and Asian markets.

YIELD: 4 SERVINGS

Sambal

4 fresh young kaffir lime leaves

½ cup minced shallot

3 red Holland or red jalapeño chiles,
    stemmed, seeded, and minced

¼ cup fresh lime juice

1 tablespoon roasted peanut oil,
    plus more for brushing

1 teaspoon sugar

½ teaspoon kosher salt

Tuna Steaks

4 (4- to 5-ounce) ahi tuna steaks

Peanut oil

Salt and pepper

To make the sambal: Using a very sharp knife, cut the lime leaves in half lengthwise, removing the center rib of the leaves. Cut the leaves very finely crosswise to make ¼-inch-long slivers. Place the leaves in a small bowl. Add the shallot, chiles, lime juice, peanut oil, sugar, and salt. *(Can be prepared to this point up to 2 hours ahead; cover and chill.)*

To grill the tuna steaks: Preheat the grill to medium-high heat. Brush both sides of the tuna steaks with oil and season with salt and pepper. Grill until the tuna steaks are not quite cooked all the way through, about 2 minutes per side. Transfer the tuna to plates, top with sambal, and serve.

Spicy Garlic and Smoked Paprika Roasted Shrimp

Smoked paprika, *pimenton de la vera*, comes in sweet (*dulce*), semi-sweet (*agro dulce*), or hot (*picante*) varieties. The red peppers that go into each variety are slowly dried over an oak fire before being ground into a powder. I prefer buying the versatile *dulce*, and adding heat with cayenne pepper—use just ¼ teaspoon cayenne for the shrimp if you prefer milder flavors. Serve the shrimp and peppers in a large bowl with toothpicks as tapas, or try it with some thick slices of crusty bread or Simple Saffron-Steamed Rice (page 161). You can also add 6 ounces of thickly sliced Spanish chorizo to the roasting pan along with the shrimp.

YIELD: 4 TO 6 SERVINGS

1 large red bell pepper

1½ pounds large (13 to 15 per pound) shrimp

3 tablespoons extra-virgin olive oil, plus more for brushing pan

8 garlic cloves, finely chopped

1½ tablespoons smoked paprika

¼ to ½ teaspoon cayenne pepper

Salt and pepper

1 tablespoon chopped fresh oregano

¼ cup dry sherry or white wine

Cut the bell pepper in half crosswise, stem and seed it, then cut it into ¾-inch thick strips.

Peel and devein the shrimp, leaving the tails intact. (*Can be prepared several hours ahead and refrigerated.*)

Preheat the oven to 400°F. Brush a heavy, large roasting pan with olive oil.

Combine the bell pepper, shrimp, garlic, paprika, cayenne pepper, and the olive oil in a large bowl and mix well. Spread the shrimp mixture out on the prepared roasting pan in a single layer. Season generously with salt and pepper.

Roast for 10 minutes. Turn the shrimp and bell pepper and sprinkle with oregano. Roast until the shrimp are just opaque in the center, about 7 minutes. Transfer to a platter.

Place the roasting pan on a burner set at medium-high heat. Add the sherry and boil, scraping up the browned bits (deglazing), about 2 minutes. Drizzle the pan juices over the shrimp mixture.

Simple Saffron Steamed Rice

2 tablespoons extra-virgin olive oil
¼ teaspoon saffron threads
2 cups long-grain white rice
1 teaspoon kosher salt

Heat the olive oil and saffron in a heavy, large saucepan over medium heat (do not burn the saffron). Add the rice and stir until the grains are coated, about 2 minutes. Add 3½ cups water and the salt and bring to a simmer. Cover and cook over very low heat until the water is absorbed and the rice is tender, about 18 minutes.

Coriander-Roasted Salmon
with Cilantro-Dill Yogurt Sauce

Tahini enriches the fresh-herb yogurt sauce in this dish, which compliments the lemon and spice-roasted salmon so well. Serve this easy-to-make entrée when entertaining, with couscous and a baby spinach salad with lemon juice and olive oil dressing.

YIELD: 6 SERVINGS

1½ tablespoons coriander seeds

Sauce

1 cup plain yogurt

2 tablespoons tahini

1 tablespoon fresh lemon juice

1 garlic clove, pressed

½ teaspoon grated lemon zest

¼ cup chopped fresh cilantro

2 tablespoons chopped fresh dill

Salt and pepper

Salmon

2 tablespoons honey

2 tablespoons fresh lemon juice

2 garlic cloves, pressed

1 tablespoon olive oil

1 teaspoon paprika

6 (5- to 6-ounce) skinless salmon fillets
    (about 1¾ inches thick)

2 large yellow bell peppers,
    cut into ½-inch strips

Salt and pepper

Cilantro

Dill sprigs

Toast the coriander seeds in a small skillet over medium heat until aromatic, stirring frequently, about 2 minutes. Remove from the heat and let the seeds cool slightly. Crush the coriander in a mortar with a pestle or coarsely grind in a spice grinder. Set aside.

To make the sauce: Stir the yogurt, tahini, lemon juice, garlic, and lemon zest together in a small bowl. Mix in 1 teaspoon of the crushed coriander, the cilantro, and dill. Season with salt and pepper to taste. *(Can be prepared to this point up to 1 day ahead.)*

To prepare the salmon: Whisk the honey, lemon juice, garlic, olive oil, paprika, and remaining crushed coriander together in a shallow baking dish. Add the salmon and turn to coat it. Cover and refrigerate for 15 minutes and up to 1 hour.

Preheat the oven to 400°F. Brush two large baking sheets with olive oil.

Transfer the salmon to one of the prepared baking sheets and the bell peppers to the other; season both with salt and pepper. Roast in the oven until the salmon is opaque in the center and the bell peppers are tender, about 10 minutes.

Transfer the peppers to a platter; top with the salmon. Garnish with cilantro and dill sprigs and serve with the yogurt sauce.

Grilled Branzino with Cannellini Bean, Herb, and Lemon Salad

A grilled fish, complete with skin and bones, head and tail even, is a delicacy all over the world, but here in the United States it's all too rare. Savoring a whole fish slowly and carefully is a treat. Branzino, a type of bass very popular in Mediterranean countries, is prized for its delicately flavored, white flesh. Known as *loup de mer* or *bar de mer* in French, branzino, as it's most often labeled, is now being farmed. Have the fish gutted and scaled at the fish market, but leave the head and the tail on!

YIELD: 2 SERVINGS

Salad

1 (15-ounce) can cannellini beans
¼ cup chopped fresh dill or flat-leaf parsley
1 green onion, sliced
2 tablespoons extra-virgin olive oil
1 tablespoon fresh lemon juice
1 tablespoon minced preserved lemon
  or 1 teaspoon grated lemon zest
1 garlic clove, pressed
¼ teaspoon crushed red pepper flakes
Salt and pepper

Fish

2 small (about 12 ounces each) branzino
  or other white-fleshed ocean fish
Olive oil
Kosher salt
Lemon slices and lemon wedges
Dill or flat-leaf parsley sprigs

To make the salad: Drain and rinse the beans. Combine the beans, dill, green onion, olive oil, lemon juice, preserved lemon, garlic, and red pepper flakes in a medium-sized bowl. Season with salt and pepper to taste.

To make the fish: Prepare the grill to medium heat.

Rub the insides and outsides of the fish with olive oil and kosher salt. Place 2 lemon slices in each fish cavity. Grill the fish until the flesh flakes easily and is opaque through to the bone when pierced with a small, sharp knife, about 5 minutes per side. Transfer the fish to two plates. Spoon the bean salad alongside the fish and garnish with lemon wedges and dill sprigs.

Preserved Meyer Lemons: *I've never met a purchased preserved lemon that I thought was worth its salt, so I make my own. Quarter 3 to 4 Meyer lemons and nestle them in two 8-ounce jars. Sprinkle with kosher salt (about 2 tablespoons per jar) between each wedge. When the lemons reach the top of the jar, press down gently to level them. Pour a ½-inch layer of extra-virgin olive oil over the lemons and seal the jar tightly. Refrigerate for at least 1 week. They'll keep until next year when a new crop of Meyer lemons is ready.*

Chicken Fricassee
with Mustard and Marjoram

Everyone loves this classic fricassee from the Dijon region of France—it's got just the right amount of kick in the mustard-flavored sauce. I like to marinate the chicken in the mustard to boost the mustard flavor of the dish, but you can skip that step if you're short on time. I serve this with oven-fried French fries or rice. A simple salad of baby frisée and a glass of red Burgundy complete the dinner beautifully.

YIELD: 4 SERVINGS

8 generous tablespoons Dijon mustard

3 tablespoons olive oil

3 tablespoons minced fresh marjoram

1 (3½-pound) whole chicken, cut into 8 pieces

Salt and pepper

1 large onion, finely chopped

4 garlic cloves, finely chopped

1 cup dry white wine

1 cup chicken broth

Stir 2 tablespoons of the mustard, 1 tablespoon of the olive oil, and 1½ tablespoons of the marjoram together in a large bowl. Add the chicken pieces, season with salt, and stir to coat. Cover and refrigerate for 2 hours or as long as overnight.

Heat the remaining 2 tablespoons olive oil in a heavy, large Dutch oven or pot over medium-high heat. Add the chicken to the pot and sprinkle with pepper. Cook until the chicken is well browned on all sides, about 12 minutes. Transfer to a bowl.

Add the onion to the pot and sauté until tender, about 8 minutes. Add the garlic and sauté for 2 minutes. Stir in the wine, broth, and remaining 6 tablespoons of mustard and 1½ tablespoon marjoram, and bring to a simmer. Return the chicken to the pot. Cover and simmer over medium-low heat until the chicken is cooked through, about 25 minutes.

Transfer the chicken to a serving dish. Boil the liquid in the pot until it has thickened to sauce consistency, about 10 minutes. Season to taste with salt and pepper and pour over the chicken.

Herb-Roasted Brined Game Hens

This is a great dish to serve at a dinner party, as you can make the herb butter and brine the hens a day before cooking. The process of brining—submerging in saltwater brine—makes the hens remarkably tender and succulent. I like to serve these hens with the Creamy Polenta (page 242) and Roasted Fennel and Carrots (page 221).

YIELD: 6 SERVINGS

½ cup kosher salt

3 Cornish game hens (about 1½ pounds each)

6 tablespoons unsalted butter, at room temperature

1 large shallot

2 garlic cloves

2 tablespoons flat-leaf parsley leaves

2 tablespoons fresh basil leaves

1 tablespoon fresh thyme

Pepper

¼ cup dry white wine

½ cup chicken broth

Flat-leaf parsley sprigs

Combine 9 cups water and the kosher salt in a deep, nonreactive pot. Stir until the salt dissolves. Submerge the hens in the brine and refrigerate for 8 to 24 hours.

Combine the butter, shallot, garlic, parsley, basil, and thyme in a food processor and process until the shallot, garlic, and herbs are very finely chopped. Season generously with pepper.

Rinse, drain, and blot the hens dry. Transfer them to a roasting pan. Carefully separate the skin from the breast, leaving the skin intact. Spread 1 generous tablespoon of herb butter under the skin and over the breast meat of each hen. Spread another generous tablespoon of herb butter over the surface of each hen. (*Can be prepared to this point up to 1 day ahead. Cover the hens and remaining herb butter with plastic wrap and refrigerate.*)

Preheat the oven to 425°F.

Roast the hens until an instant-read thermometer inserted into the thickest part of the thigh registers 175°F., about 40 minutes. Transfer the hens to a platter.

Cook the remaining herb butter in a heavy, medium-sized saucepan until fragrant, about 1 minute. Add the wine and boil until the mixture is reduced by half, about 2 minutes. Add the chicken broth and any pan juices and boil until the mixture is reduced to 1¼ cups, about 2 minutes.

Using kitchen shears, cut the hens in half and arrange them on the platter. Garnish the platter with parsley and serve with the pan juices.

Moroccan Chicken Skewers

For convenience, I keep flash-frozen, boneless, skinless chicken thighs in my freezer. They can be quickly defrosted in a ziptop bag in a large bowl of cold water. Serve the chicken with Cous Cous with Barberries and Mint (page 238) or warm pita bread and grilled zucchini.

YIELD: 6 SERVINGS

Marinade

1 small onion, quartered
¼ cup fresh lemon juice
¼ cup extra-virgin olive oil
2-inch piece fresh ginger, peeled and sliced
4 garlic cloves
2 tablespoons ground cumin
1 tablespoon caraway seeds
1 tablespoon sambal oelek
  or ½ teaspoon crushed red pepper flakes
1 tablespoon paprika
1 teaspoon kosher salt
1 pinch saffron threads

Chicken

2½ pounds boneless, skinless chicken
  thighs, cut into 1½-inch pieces
Salt and pepper
Chopped fresh flat-leaf parsley or cilantro

To make the marinade: Purée the marinade ingredients in a food processor until smooth.

Thread the chicken onto bamboo skewers and place them in a large baking dish. Pour the marinade over the chicken and turn to coat well. Cover with plastic and refrigerate overnight.

To make the chicken: Preheat the grill to medium heat.

Season the chicken with salt and pepper and grill until no longer pink and cooked through, turning frequently, about 10 minutes.

Transfer the skewers to a platter. Sprinkle with parsley and serve.

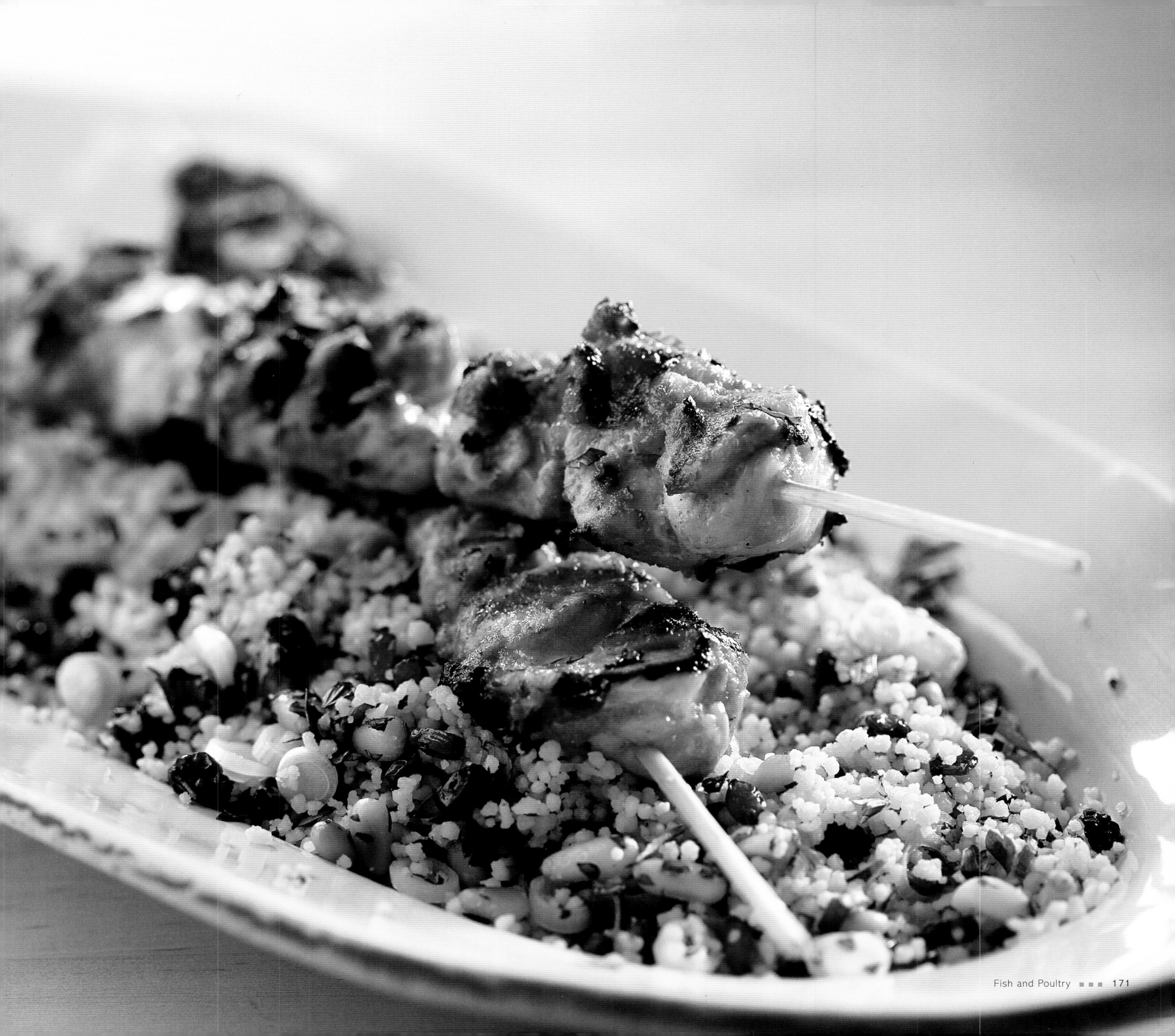

Updated Chicken Piccata

This dish updates an old-fashioned lemon and caper favorite that's usually made with veal, by adding a fresh herb topping of flat-leaf parsley, basil leaves, and Pecorino Romano cheese.

YIELD: 4 TO 6 SERVINGS

¼ cup flat-leaf parsley leaves

¼ cup torn basil leaves

¼ cup drained capers

4 tablespoons extra-virgin olive oil

4 tablespoons minced shallots

4 (6- to 7-ounce) boneless chicken breasts, skin on

Salt and pepper

4 garlic cloves, minced

⅔ cup dry white wine

1 tablespoon fresh lemon juice

½ cup coarsely grated Pecorino Romano cheese

Preheat the oven to 400°F.

Combine the parsley, basil, and capers in a small bowl. Mix in 2 tablespoons of the olive oil and 1 tablespoon of the shallots.

Sprinkle both sides of the chicken breasts with salt and pepper. Heat the remaining 2 tablespoons olive oil in a heavy, large skillet over medium-high heat. Add the chicken breasts, skin-side down and sear until golden brown, about 6 minutes. Turn and cook the second side until golden brown, about 3 minutes longer. Transfer the chicken to a small roasting pan. Roast the chicken breasts in the oven until just cooked through, about 5 minutes.

Meanwhile, add the remaining 3 tablespoons shallots and the garlic to the skillet and sauté over medium heat until tender, about 1 minute. Add the wine and lemon juice, and simmer until the mixture is reduced to ½ cup, about 2 minutes.

Transfer the chicken to a platter. Stir any juices from the roasting pan into the wine sauce and season with salt and pepper to taste. Pour the sauce over the chicken. Toss the parsley mixture with the cheese and season generously with pepper. Top each chicken breast with the parsley mixture and serve.

Whole-Spice Chicken Curry

I don't know what style this curry is or what country it hails from, but I do know that it was inspired by the lime leaf tree and bay shrubs in my backyard. The dish is served complete with whole spices, as it is in India. I love the depth of flavor that they provide. But be sure to advise your guests to move them aside as they enjoy the curry. This is another great dish for entertaining, as you can make it entirely ahead of time, and the chicken actually gets better as it sits. Serve with the Bay Leaf–Scented Rice Pilaf (page 241) or steamed rice.

YIELD: 6 TO 8 SERVINGS

2 tablespoons unsalted butter or vegetable oil

2 onions, finely chopped

8 garlic cloves, minced

2 tablespoons finely grated fresh ginger

2 bay leaves, preferably fresh

2 kaffir lime leaves

1 cinnamon stick

6 whole green cardamom pods, lightly crushed

1 teaspoon cumin seeds

1 teaspoon ground turmeric

4 whole cloves

⅛ teaspoon crushed red pepper flakes

12 skinless chicken thighs with bones (about 4 pounds)

Salt and pepper

2 cups chicken broth

1 (14-ounce) can light coconut milk

Melt the butter in a heavy, large Dutch oven over medium heat. Add the onions and sauté until very tender, about 8 minutes. Add the garlic, ginger, bay leaves, lime leaves, cinnamon stick, cardamon pods, cumin seeds, turmeric, cloves, and red pepper flakes, and cook for 2 minutes. Add the chicken and cook just until it is no longer pink, turning once, about 4 minutes.

Sprinkle the chicken with salt and pepper. Add the chicken broth and coconut milk and stir gently. Cover and simmer over medium-low heat for 10 minutes. Uncover and continue simmering the chicken over low heat until it is very tender and the sauce is thick, about 1 hour. (*Can be prepared up to 2 days ahead. Cool, cover, and refrigerate. Reheat over medium-low heat, stirring occasionally until the chicken is heated through.*)

Lemon-Roasted Chicken with Potatoes, Olives, and Oregano

A roast chicken is a comforting dinner that is special enough for guests. I like to make Roasted Baby Artichokes (page 228) when I cook this dish since they both roast at the same temperature. They go great with the tender chicken and potatoes. Rubbing olive oil and mixed herbs under the chicken skin keeps the bird moist and flavorful. While the sumac is a fun, tart addition, the chicken still shines without it.

YIELD: 4 TO 6 SERVINGS

2 lemons

4 tablespoons chopped fresh oregano

4 garlic cloves, minced

3 tablespoons extra-virgin olive oil, plus more for brushing

1 (5- to 5¼-pound) roasting chicken

Salt and pepper

1 generous teaspoon ground sumac, optional

1¼ pounds baby potatoes (about 1-inch round)

½ cup pitted kalamata olives

1 cup chicken broth

Lemon wedges

Preheat the oven to 400°F. Brush a 15 x 10-inch roasting pan with olive oil.

Zest the lemons, then cut them in half and juice them. Set aside the juice, zest, and lemon halves separately.

Combine 3 tablespoons of the oregano, three-fourths of the garlic cloves, the olive oil, and half the lemon zest in a small bowl and mix well. Place the chicken in the prepared pan. Slide your hand under the skin of the chicken breast to loosen it from the breast meat. Spoon approximately 1 tablespoon of the oregano-garlic mixture under the skin of each breast. Press down on the skin to distribute the mixture evenly. Rub the remaining mixture over the entire surface of the chicken. Season the chicken generously with salt and pepper. Sprinkle with sumac. Place the reserved lemon halves in the cavity of the chicken and tie the legs together with kitchen string. Roast the chicken for 20 minutes.

Reduce the oven temperature to 350°F. Add the potatoes to the pan and stir to coat with the pan drippings. Roast for 30 minutes.

Add the olives and sprinkle with the remaining oregano, garlic, and lemon zest. Season the potatoes with salt and pepper and stir to combine. Continue roasting until an internal thermometer registers 160°F. when inserted into the thickest part of the chicken thigh and the vegetables are tender, about 10 minutes longer.

Transfer the chicken to a platter. Using a slotted spoon, surround the chicken with the potatoes and olives. Add the chicken broth and 2 tablespoons of the lemon juice to the drippings in the pan and simmer over medium heat, stirring up the browned bits, until the sauce is lightly reduced and flavorful, about 2 minutes. Season the sauce with salt and pepper to taste, adding more lemon juice, if desired. Serve the sauce with the chicken and garnish with lemon wedges.

Stuffed Turkey Breast with Achiote, Poblano Chiles, and Feta Cheese

This is a good dish for a dinner party as it doubles easily and can be assembled a day before roasting—and it looks impressive when sliced. Serve it as part of a buffet with Black Beans with Orange and Chipotle (page 236), which can also be made ahead. To make things easier, buy a boned turkey breast (about 1¾ to 2 pounds). Achiote is the slightly musky-flavored seed of the annatto tree. Although it adds color and flavor to the turkey, it can be left out.

YIELD: 4 TO 6 SERVINGS

3 fresh poblano chiles

¼ cup olive oil

4 garlic cloves, finely chopped

1 tablespoon ground cumin

1 teaspoon ground achiote powder or annatto

2¼ to 2⅓ pound turkey breast half with ribs attached

Salt and pepper

4 ounces crumbled feta cheese

3 tablespoons chopped fresh oregano

1 cup chicken broth

½ cup dry white wine

Char the chiles over a gas flame or in the broiler until blackened all over. Transfer them to a bowl and cover with plastic, allowing the chiles to steam while cooling. Peel, stem, and seed the chiles. *(Can be prepared to this point up to 2 days ahead. Cover and refrigerate.)*

Whisk the oil, garlic, cumin, and achiote together in a small bowl.

Using a small sharp knife, remove the bones from the turkey breast; set the bones aside. Place the turkey meat between two sheets of plastic wrap and pound it with a mallet to flatten it to a rough 12 x 9-inch rectangle, ½-inch thick. Remove the top sheet of plastic. Brush the turkey with half the garlic mixture and season with salt and pepper. Top the turkey evenly with the chiles. Sprinkle with feta and 2 tablespoons of the oregano. Starting at one long side, roll up the turkey, jelly-roll style, tucking the ends in, to create an approximately 10 x 4-inch roast. Tie the roast with kitchen twine in several places to secure.

Brush a heavy, large metal baking pan with olive oil. Transfer the turkey to the pan and brush with the remaining garlic mixture. Nestle the reserved bones alongside the turkey and sprinkle both with salt and pepper. *(Can be prepared to this point up to 1 day ahead; wrap in plastic wrap and refrigerate.)*

Preheat the oven to 400°F.

Roast the turkey until an internal meat thermometer registers 160°F, about 40 minutes.

Transfer the turkey to a cutting board, tent it with aluminum foil, and let it stand for 10 minutes.

Add the broth and wine to the baking pan and boil over high heat, stirring up the browned bits until the liquid is reduced to 1 cup, about 5 minutes. Discard the bones and stir in the remaining 1 tablespoon oregano. Season the sauce to taste with salt and pepper.

Remove the strings from the turkey and slice it into rounds. Arrange the slices on a platter and drizzle with the sauce.

Duck Breasts with Quince Sauce

Quince is an ancient tree fruit that looks like a cross between an apple and a pear. It has a lovely perfume—I often place a quince on the ledge in my kitchen in the fall so I can enjoy the fragrance. In this dish, *membrillo*, Spanish quince paste, is used to make the sauce for the seared duck breasts, resulting in a sweet, sophisticated, deeply flavored sauce. *Membrillo* is an orange-brown-colored firm gel made from quince. It contains a high amount of pectin, honey, and spices. In Spain, it's traditionally served with cheese. You can find it at cheese shops, specialty food markets, Spanish markets, and online. Duck breasts can vary greatly in size—if you can't find small ones, use fewer large ones.

YIELD: 4 SERVINGS

1 ½ cups chicken broth

3 ounces *membrillo* (about ⅓ cup)

4 small or 2 large boneless duck breasts (about 1¾ pounds total)

Salt and pepper

¼ cup minced shallot

1 large garlic clove, minced

½ cup dry white wine

Combine the chicken broth and membrillo in a blender and purée until smooth.

Place the duck skin-side down in a heavy, large skillet over medium heat. Cook the duck, without moving it, until the fat renders from the skin and the skin becomes golden brown, about 15 minutes. Pour off the fat occasionally.

Season the meat side of the duck breasts with salt and pepper. Loosen the duck from the pan with a spatula. Increase the heat to medium-high and continue cooking the duck, skin-side down, until the skin is thin and browned, about 4 minutes. Turn the duck and continue cooking until it is cooked to medium doneness, about 4 minutes longer. Transfer the duck to a plate.

Pour off all but about 1 tablespoon of the fat from the skillet. Add the shallot and garlic and sauté for 1 minute. Add the wine and cook, stirring up the browned bits, (deglazing) until the liquid evaporates, about 3 minutes. Add the membrillo mixture and boil until the sauce thickens slightly and is reduced to 1 cup, about 7 minutes. Pour any juices from the duck into the sauce. Season with salt and pepper to taste.

Thinly slice the duck (if desired) and arrange on plates. Spoon the sauce over the duck and serve.

Cooking with Duck Fat

Duck fat is highly valued in France for its flavor and low level of saturated fats. Many cooks, French and otherwise, save duck fat for the sole purpose of cooking potatoes. Here is a simple method for roasting potatoes in duck fat.

Peel 2 pounds of small (1½- to 2-inch round) new potatoes and boil them in salted water until they are just tender, about 15 minutes. Drain well. Spread the potatoes out on a baking sheet to dry. (Can be prepared to this point up to 1 day ahead. Cover the potatoes and refrigerate.) Toss the potatoes with ⅓ cup duck fat and arrange in a single layer on a heavy roasting pan. Season with salt and pepper and roast in a 450°F. oven until golden brown, stirring once, about 20 minutes.

Meats

Grilled Skirt Steak Tacos with Rajas con Crema

Rajas con crema are roasted green chiles stewed in cream. The rich Mexican condiment is perfect with the red chile–rubbed steak, but it also makes really good tacos when paired with black beans and warm corn tortillas. A skirt steak is a long, flat cut of beef from the flank. The flavorful cut is sometimes labeled "fajita steak," since it is often used to make fajitas. Some markets label the dark-green poblano chiles as pasilla peppers.

YIELD: 12 TACOS; 4 SERVINGS

Rajas

4 poblano chiles

1 tablespoon olive oil

1 large onion, sliced

4 garlic cloves, chopped

⅓ cup heavy cream

2 tablespoons chopped fresh oregano
   or 1 teaspoon dried, crumbled

Salt

Steak

1 tablespoon mild ground red chile
   (such as ancho, California, or New Mexico)

1 tablespoon ground cumin

2 teaspoons kosher salt

1 pound skirt steak

1 dozen corn tortillas, warmed

Chopped fresh cilantro

To make the rajas: Char the chiles over a gas flame or under a broiler until blackened and charred on all sides. Transfer the chiles to a bowl and cover with plastic, allowing the peppers to steam while cooling. Peel, seed, stem, and slice the chiles.

Heat the oil in a heavy, medium-sized skillet over medium heat. Add the onion and sauté until tender and golden, about 15 minutes. Stir in the garlic and sauté for 2 minutes. Add the chiles and ¾ cup water, and cook until the onion and chiles are very tender and the water evaporates, about 8 minutes. Stir in the cream and oregano and bring to a simmer. Cook just until the chiles are coated with cream, about 1 minute. Season with salt to taste. *(Can be prepared to this point up to 3 days ahead; refrigerate. Reheat in the microwave or by stirring over medium heat.)*

To prepare the steak: Combine the chile, cumin, and salt in a small bowl. Sprinkle both sides of the steak with the chile mixture, rubbing it into the meat with your fingertips.

Preheat the grill to high heat. Grill the steak until it is still pink in center, 2 to 3 minutes per side. Transfer the steak to a cutting board and cut it across the grain into thin strips.

To serve, divide the meat evenly among the tortillas. Top with the rajas, sprinkle with cilantro, and serve.

My favorite warm tortillas: *Place a tortilla directly over a gas flame until it is very lightly charred at the edges, about 5 seconds. Turn the tortilla and lightly char the second side. Wrap in aluminum foil to keep warm. Repeat with the remaining tortillas. Use the tortillas immediately or place the foil-wrapped tortillas in the toaster oven and keep warm.*

Grilled Top Sirloin
with Jeanne's Secret Marinade

Top sirloin is my favorite steak. It may not be as tender as high-end cuts like rib-eye and New York, but you can't beat the flavor of this juicy cut. Top sirloin is especially tasty with my "secret" fusion marinade. This recipe doubles, triples, even quadruples to serve a crowd. Potatoes and green salad are perfect accompaniments. Pomegranate molasses is a sweet-tart pomegranate concentrate that is available at Middle Eastern Markets. Bufalo brand chipotle hot sauce can be found in the Mexican food aisle at the supermarket and at Mexican markets.

YIELD: 4 SERVINGS

⅓ cup soy sauce

3 tablespoons pomegranate molasses

1 tablespoon chipotle hot sauce, such as Bufalo brand

2 garlic cloves, pressed

1 pound boneless top sirloin steak, preferably aged prime (about 1½-inches thick)

Mix the soy sauce, pomegranate molasses, hot sauce, and garlic together in a shallow baking dish. Add the steak and turn to coat it. Cover and refrigerate for 8 hours or overnight, turning the meat occasionally.

Prepare the grill to medium-high heat. Grill the steak for about 4 minutes per side for medium-rare doneness. Transfer the steak to a cutting board and let it stand for 10 minutes. Thinly slice the steak crosswise and serve.

"One Cow" Burgers

If you've read either *Fast Food Nation*, by Eric Schlosser, or *The Omnivore's Dilemma* by Michael Pollan, you probably know that if you buy ground beef or preformed hamburger patties from the grocery store, you'll end up with meat that is a mixture of many, possibly hundreds of cows. Regardless of the safety issues with so many cows in the mix, it just doesn't sit right, taste-wise, on the bun. Butchers, even the ones who work at the big chain markets, are more than happy to grind a piece of chuck for you, ensuring that your burger not only tastes better, but comes from only one cow. I like to keep the toppings on my hamburgers pretty simple, letting the superior meat flavor stand out, but a thin slice of sharp white cheddar is tasty when slightly melted atop the patty.

YIELD: 6 BURGERS

Burgers

2 pounds freshly ground chuck roast

2 teaspoons chopped fresh thyme

2 garlic cloves, pressed

1 teaspoon salt, plus more to taste

1 teaspoon coarsely ground pepper,
    plus more to taste

1 rounded teaspoon bacon grease
    or unsalted butter

Unsalted butter, at room temperature

6 hamburger buns

Optional Toppings

Lettuce leaves

Sliced red onion

Sliced tomato

Pickles (I like bread-and-butter pickles)

Ketchup

Dijon mustard

Combine the beef with the thyme, garlic, salt, and pepper in a large bowl and mix well. Form the beef into six 4-inch patties, about 5 ounces each. *(Can be prepared to this point up to 2 days ahead. Wrap the patties in plastic and refrigerate.)*

Heat the bacon grease in a heavy, large skillet over medium high heat. Season the patties with additional salt and pepper. Cook the patties, in batches if necessary, until browned on both sides, turning once, about 6 minutes total for medium-rare doneness. (To grill the burgers: Prepare the grill to medium-high heat. Grill the patties until they are browned, turning once, about 8 minutes for medium-rare.)

Meanwhile, preheat the broiler.

Lightly butter the buns and arrange them, buttered side up on a heavy, large baking pan. Broil until they are lightly toasted. Transfer the cooked burgers to the bottom halves of the buns. Add desired toppings and serve.

Beef Short Ribs with Red Wine, Cipollini, and Herbes de Provence

Every time I make short ribs for friends, I'm surprised at how many ask for the recipe—I guess I'm not the only one who enjoys the rich, full flavor of slow-cooked beef. Make the short ribs ahead if you want and serve them with mashed potatoes. Cipollinis, sometimes called "wild onions," taste like sweet, delicate onions, but they're actually not onions at all—they are the bulbs of the grape hyacinth.

YIELD: 8 SERVINGS

1 tablespoon olive oil

4½ pounds meaty beef short ribs, cut into 3- to 4-inch lengths

Salt and pepper

1 onion, chopped

1 pound carrots, peeled and sliced

6 garlic cloves, chopped

1 (28-ounce) can diced tomatoes

2 cups dry red wine

1 cup beef broth or water

4 bay leaves, preferably fresh

1 tablespoon herbes de Provence

1 pound cipollini, peeled

Preheat the oven to 325°F.

Heat the olive oil in a heavy, large Dutch oven over medium-high heat. Season the ribs with salt and pepper, and add to the Dutch oven. Cook the ribs, turning occasionally, until they are well browned on all sides, about 15 minutes.

Transfer the ribs to a bowl. Pour off all but a thin layer of fat from the Dutch oven. Add the chopped onion and carrots, and sauté until golden brown, about 8 minutes. Stir in the garlic. Add the tomatoes with their juices, the red wine, broth, bay leaves, and herbes de Provence. Bring the mixture to a simmer, stirring up any browned bits from the bottom of the Dutch oven.

Return the ribs to the Dutch oven, nestling them into the vegetable mixture. Add the cipollini. Season with salt and pepper to taste. Cover and cook in the oven until the ribs are very tender when pierced with a fork and the liquid has thickened to a sauce, about 2½ hours. Stir carefully once or twice while cooking and add additional broth or water if the sauce becomes too thick or appears dry. *(Can be prepared up to 2 days ahead. Cover and refrigerate. Remove any solidified fat from the ribs. Reheat in a 350°F. oven, stirring occasionally and adding additional broth or water if necessary, about 1 hour.)*

Tamarind Pork Ribs

The tamarind tree is native to Africa and grows in tropical climates. The tamarind's brown pods contain a sticky, tart pulp and seeds. The pulp is used in Indian, Latin, and Asian cuisines. Most Americans are familiar with tamarind in the form of Worcestershire sauce. I like to use Indian tamarind paste in this Caribbean-style dish because it is so concentrated and creates such a wonderful sweet-tart sauce that's like an exotic version of American-style barbecue sauce. For the best flavor, choose a seedless concentrated paste that is the color of soy sauce with the consistency of molasses. Neera's, Mr. Manish, and Tamicon are all good brands that are available at specialty food stores, Indian markets, or online. Serve these ribs with the Fresh Bay Leaf Scented–Rice Pilaf (page 241) and the Black Beans with Orange and Chipotle (page 236) for a Latin-flavored feast.

YIELD: 6 TO 8 SERVINGS

½ cup light brown sugar, firmly packed

3½ tablespoons seedless tamarind paste

6 garlic cloves, chopped

2 tablespoons finely grated fresh ginger

2 tablespoons chopped fresh oregano

1 tablespoon coriander seeds, coarsely ground

1 teaspoon kosher salt

½ teaspoon crushed red pepper flakes

2 racks baby back pork ribs (4 to 5 pounds total), cut in half

Chopped fresh cilantro

Combine the brown sugar, tamarind paste, garlic, ginger, oregano, coriander seeds, salt, red pepper flakes, and 3 cups water in a heavy Dutch oven or a deep skillet and bring to a simmer over medium-high heat, stirring until the sugar and tamarind paste dissolve. Reduce the heat to medium-low. Add the ribs, cover, and simmer until tender, about 30 minutes, moving the ribs once or twice. *(Can be prepared to this point up to 3 days ahead. Cool, cover, and refrigerate the ribs in the cooking liquid. Remove any solidified fat before continuing.)*

Using a sharp knife, cut the pork between the bones into single ribs. Return the ribs to the cooking liquid. Simmer uncovered over medium heat until the ribs are very tender and the liquid is thickened and reduced to a glaze, about 40 minutes.

Transfer the ribs to a platter, sprinkle with cilantro, and serve.

Brined Pork Chops with Apples and Sage

When I was a little girl, I always got to pick what I wanted for dinner on my birthday. Even as a kid, I must have been tuned in to eating seasonally—my birthday is in January, and I always wanted pork chops with applesauce. In this recipe, I gussy up the classic apple and pork combo with allspice brine (to keep the pork moist), sautéed apples, and gravy made with freshly pressed apple juice. The fresh apple juice really makes a difference in the flavor: you can find it at farmers' markets or in the refrigerated section of the market.

YIELD: 4 SERVINGS

2 tablespoons kosher salt

2 teaspoons whole allspice, cracked or 1 teaspoon ground

4 center-cut pork rib chops (about 2 pounds total)

4 tablespoons unsalted butter

3 Golden Delicious apples, peeled, cored, and cut into eighths

Salt and pepper

⅓ cup finely chopped shallot

18 fresh sage leaves, coarsely chopped

2 tablespoons Calvados or apple brandy

1¼ to 1½ cups fresh-pressed apple juice

1 cup chicken broth

2 teaspoons unbleached all-purpose flour

In a baking dish large enough to hold the pork chops in a single layer, stir 4 cups water, the salt, and allspice together until the salt dissolves. Submerge the pork chops in the brine and refrigerate overnight.

Melt 2 tablespoons of the butter in a heavy, large skillet over medium heat. Add the apples and sauté until golden and just tender, about 10 minutes. Transfer the apples to a platter and cover with aluminum foil to keep warm.

Meanwhile, drain the pork chops and pat them dry. Season the pork with freshly cracked pepper. Melt 1 tablespoon of the butter in the same skillet over medium-high heat. Add the pork chops and cook until they are well browned on both sides and just cooked through, turning once, about 3 minutes per side. Transfer the pork chops to the platter with the apples and keep warm.

Add ½ tablespoon butter to the skillet, then add the shallot and half the sage and stir briefly to soften the shallot, about 30 seconds. Add the Calvados and boil until almost dry, about 1 minute. Pour in 1¼ cups apple juice and the chicken broth and bring to a boil. Boil until the mixture is reduced to 1 cup, about 8 minutes. Transfer the mixture to a measuring cup.

Melt the remaining ½ tablespoon butter in the same skillet over medium heat. Add the flour and the remaining sage and stir for 30 seconds (do not brown the flour). Return the apple juice mixture to the skillet and stir until the mixture boils and thickens, about 1 minute.

Return the apples and pork to the skillet and stir to coat them with the sauce, adding the remaining ¼ cup apple juice to thin the sauce if necessary. Transfer to plates and serve.

Roast Pork Tenderloin with Smoked Paprika, Potatoes, and Haricots Verts

Roasting at high heat is a great way to maximize flavor in meats and vegetables. With this recipe, everything is cooked in the same pan, resulting in an impressive, complete meal that takes only minutes to prepare with minimal cleanup. *Haricots verts* is French for green beans and the French variety is thinner and smaller than regular green beans (which can be used in this recipe, too). Smoked paprika, a product from eastern Spain, adds a wonderful smoky-spiced flavor to the dish.

YIELD: 4 SERVINGS

1 pound baby potatoes, quartered

4 tablespoons olive oil, plus more for brushing the pan

Salt and pepper

1 generous tablespoon smoked paprika

4 garlic cloves, pressed

1 tablespoon fresh oregano or 1 teaspoon dried

1 pound pork tenderloin

10 ounces trimmed haricots verts or baby green beans

¼ cup dry white wine

¼ cup chicken broth

Preheat the oven to 450°F. Brush a heavy, large shallow roasting pan with olive oil.

In the prepared pan, toss the potatoes with 1 tablespoon olive oil, and season with salt and pepper. Roast for 5 minutes.

Meanwhile, mix the remaining 3 tablespoons olive oil, paprika, garlic, and oregano in a small bowl. Coat the pork evenly with half the paprika mixture and season it with salt and pepper. Transfer the pork to the roasting pan with the potatoes and continue roasting until the pork is almost cooked, about 15 minutes, stirring the potatoes occasionally.

Toss the haricots verts with half the remaining paprika mixture and season with salt and pepper. Add them to the roasting pan, surrounding the pork and potatoes. Drizzle the potatoes with the remaining paprika mixture, stir, and continue roasting until an instant-read thermometer inserted into the center of the pork registers 140°F and the green beans are crisp-tender, about 5 minutes longer.

Transfer the pork to a cutting board and the potatoes and green beans to a platter. Add the wine and broth to the roasting pan and return it to the oven. Turn the oven off and leave the roasting pan in the oven to allow the wine mixture to reduce slightly.

Slice the pork and arrange on the platter with the green beans and potatoes. Stir the broth mixture, scraping the browned bits from the roasting pan. Season with salt and pepper and pour over the pork.

Pork Chops with Grilled Nectarines

This makes an easy summer supper when served with corn on the cob, a green salad, and a glass of chilled Spanish rosé. I like to use thin pork chops because they cook quickly and you get more of the grilled herb and spice flavor per bite. The nectarines can be substituted with peaches for equally delicious results.

YIELD: 4 SERVINGS

1 tablespoon minced fresh marjoram
1 garlic clove, pressed
½ teaspoon ground allspice
4 pork loin chops (about ½ inch thick)
Salt and pepper
4 firm-ripe nectarines, cut in half
Olive oil
Marjoram sprigs, optional

Prepare the grill to medium heat.

Combine the marjoram, garlic, and allspice in a small bowl. Rub the garlic mixture over both sides of the pork chops. Season with salt and pepper to taste. Grill the pork until it is browned and cooked through, about 4 minutes per side.

Brush the nectarines lightly with olive oil and season with salt and pepper. Grill the nectarines until just tender, turning occasionally, about 6 minutes.

Place the pork chops on a platter and surround them with the nectarines. Garnish with marjoram sprigs and serve.

Spiced Lamb with Mint, Date, and Apple-Pear Relish

Roasted spiced lamb is so delicious with the sweet, fresh fruit relish, I've included two options for your choice cut of lamb: roasted rack of lamb and a grilled butterflied leg of lamb. Try both or either for great results. For the relish, use a dry, firm date such as a Deglet Noor for easy chopping. The Asian apple-pear adds a unique, juicy crunch and sweet, floral flavor to the relish. Find them at the supermarket where they are sometimes labeled Japanese or Chinese pears. This Moroccan-influenced dish is great served with the Couscous with Currants, Barberries, and Mint (page 238) and the Carrot Salad with Green Olives and Green Onions (page 91).

YIELD: LEG OF LAMB, ABOUT 8 SERVINGS;
          RACK OF LAMB, 4 TO 6 SERVINGS

Spice Blend

2 tablespoons cumin seeds

2 tablespoons coriander seeds

2 (2½-inch) cinnamon sticks, broken in half

2 tablespoons paprika

1 teaspoon turmeric

½ teaspoon cayenne pepper

Relish

3 tablespoons orange juice

2 tablespoons extra-virgin olive oil

1 tablespoon pomegranate molasses

1 garlic clove, pressed

4 green onions, finely sliced

½ cup chopped fresh mint leaves

¼ cup chopped flat-leaf parsley

1 small Asian apple-pear,
   peeled, cored, and diced

⅔ cup chopped dates
   (about 10 pitted dates)

Salt and pepper

Rack of lamb

2 racks of lamb (about 1½ pounds each)
   well-trimmed

Olive oil

2 large garlic cloves, pressed

Salt and pepper

Mint sprigs, optional

Leg of lamb

4-pound boneless, butterflied leg of lamb,
   trimmed of fat and sinew

Olive oil

4 large garlic cloves, pressed

Salt and pepper

Mint sprigs, optional

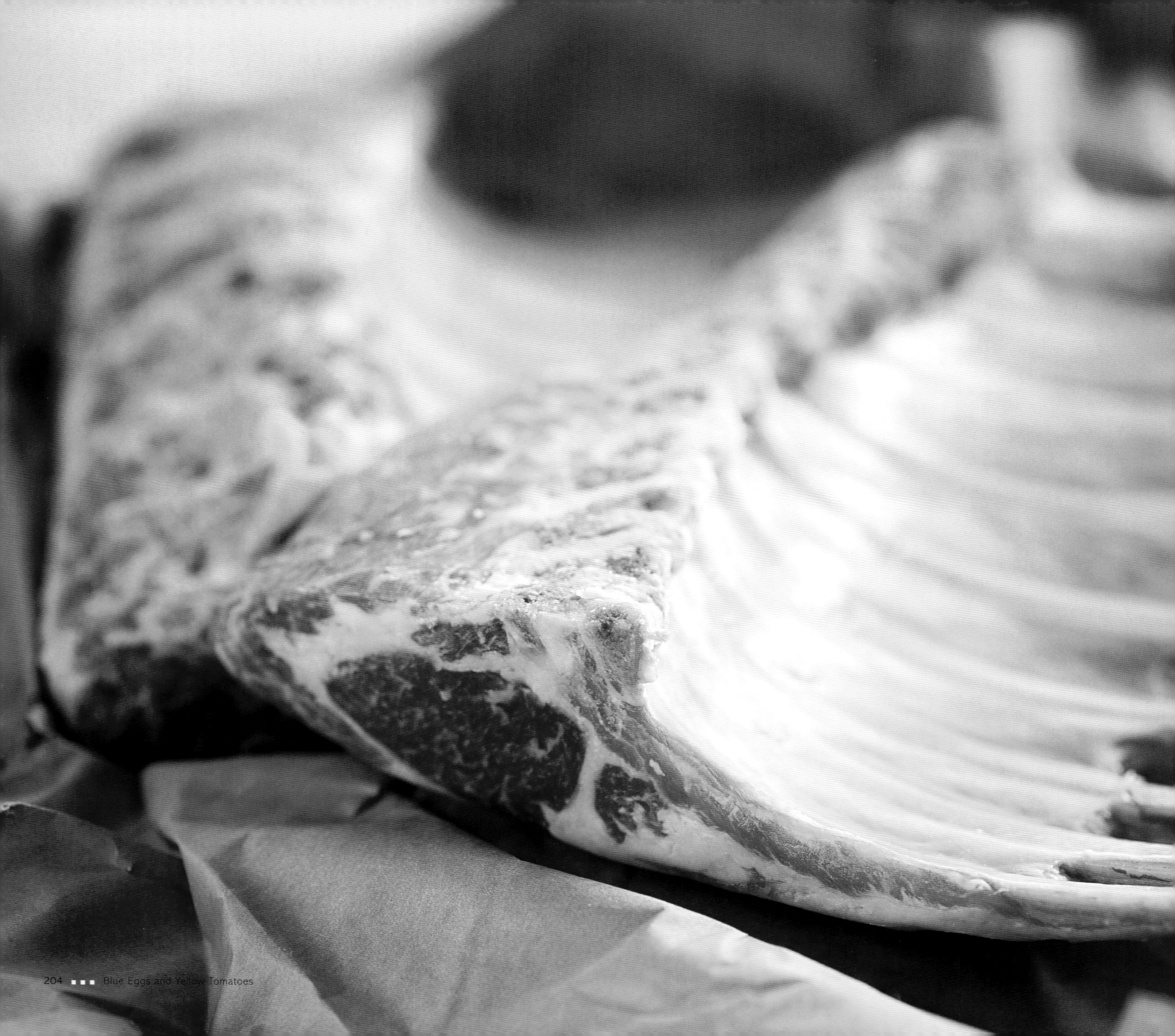

To make the spice blend: Toast the cumin seeds, coriander seeds, and cinnamon sticks in a heavy, medium-sized skillet over medium-high heat until fragrant, about 2 minutes. Cool the spices and transfer them to a spice mill or coffee grinder. Finely grind the spices and transfer to a small bowl. Mix in the paprika, turmeric, and cayenne pepper. *(The spice blend can be prepared up to 2 weeks ahead. Store in an airtight container.)*

To make the relish: Whisk the orange juice, olive oil, pomegranate molasses, and garlic together in a medium-sized bowl. Mix in the green onions, mint, and parsley. Fold the apple-pear and dates into the herb mixture. Season with salt and pepper to taste.

To prepare the rack of lamb: Preheat the oven to 450°F.

Place the lamb on a heavy baking sheet and rub it with olive oil and garlic. Season the lamb generously with salt and pepper. Sprinkle with enough spice blend to coat it completely. *(The rack of lamb can be prepared to this point up to 1 day ahead. Cover and refrigerate.)*

Roast the lamb until an instant-read thermometer registers 130°F. for medium-rare doneness, about 15 minutes. Let the lamb stand for 10 minutes.

Cut the lamb between the ribs into chops. Arrange the chops on plates and garnish with mint sprigs. Serve with the relish.

To prepare the leg of lamb: Preheat the oven to 450°F.

Place the lamb in a large baking dish and rub it with olive oil and garlic. Season the lamb generously with salt and pepper. Sprinkle the spice blend evenly over the lamb to coat completely. *(The leg of lamb can be prepared to this point up to 1 day ahead. Cover and refrigerate.)*

Prepare the grill to medium heat.

Grill the lamb, turning once, until an instant-read thermometer registers 130°F. for medium-rare doneness, about 8 minutes per side.

Transfer the lamb to a carving board and let it stand for 15 minutes. Thinly slice the lamb and arrange it on a platter. Garnish with mint sprigs and serve with relish.

Slow-Roasted Leg of Lamb with Rosemary, Garlic, and Fingerling Potatoes

This is a simple roast that is great for a family supper. There's a lot of garlic, but the long, slow roasting mellows its flavor beautifully. Fingerling potatoes are new potatoes with an elongated shape—they look a bit like fat, gnarly fingers. Fingerlings have a rich and nutty flavor with a smooth and creamy texture. They come in several varieties: Rose Finn Apple, Russian Banana, Princess Larate, and French Fingerling. If you can't find one of these varieties, use baby new potatoes.

YIELD: 6 TO 8 SERVINGS

20 garlic cloves, peeled

2½ tablespoons fresh rosemary leaves

Salt and pepper

4-pound semi-boneless leg of lamb roast

2 tablespoons olive oil

1 cup sweet vermouth or Madeira

2½ cups beef broth

1½ pounds fingerling potatoes

Preheat the oven to 325°F.

Mince 3 garlic cloves with 1 tablespoon of rosemary leaves. Rub the lamb with the garlic mixture and season with salt and pepper.

Heat the olive oil in a heavy, large Dutch oven over medium-high heat. Add the lamb and cook until it is browned on all sides, about 10 minutes. Add the vermouth and bring to a simmer. Add 2 cups of the beef broth, 1 tablespoon of the rosemary leaves and the remaining garlic. Cover and roast until the meat is tender when pierced with a knife, about 2½ hours.

Add the potatoes and ¼- to ½-cup additional broth if the bottom of the Dutch oven appears dry. Cover and continue roasting until the lamb and potatoes are very tender, about 30 minutes. Transfer the lamb to a cutting board and slice. Arrange the potatoes and lamb slices on a platter; sprinkle with the remaining rosemary. Serve with the pan juices.

Braised Lamb Shanks with Tomato, Lemon Zest, and Rosemary

Braising is slow, moist cooking. The long, gentle simmer breaks down the connective tissue in tougher cuts of meat resulting in a rich, unctuous sauce. I love to serve this hearty dish with the Creamy Polenta on page 242.

YIELD: 4 SERVINGS

1½ tablespoons olive oil

4 lamb shanks (about 12 ounces each)

1 large onion, chopped

2 carrots, peeled and chopped

6 garlic cloves, chopped

1 (28-ounce) can diced tomatoes

1½ cups dry white wine

2 tablespoons chopped fresh rosemary

1 tablespoon plus 1 teaspoon grated lemon zest

1 teaspoon crushed red pepper flakes

½ teaspoon salt

Heat the oil in a heavy, large Dutch oven over medium heat. Add the lamb shanks and cook until browned on all sides, turning occasionally, about 12 minutes. Transfer the shanks to a bowl.

Add the onion, carrots, and garlic to the Dutch oven and sauté until the onions begin to brown, about 8 minutes. Stir in the tomatoes and their juices, the wine, 1½ cups water, 1 tablespoon of the rosemary, 1 tablespoon of the lemon zest, the red pepper flakes, and salt. Bring the mixture to a boil.

Return the lamb shanks to the pot. Reduce the heat to low, cover, and simmer gently over low heat until the lamb is tender, stirring occasionally, about 2½ hours.

Uncover and simmer until the lamb is very tender and the liquid reduces to a sauce consistency, about 1 hour. (Can be prepared up to 2 days ahead. Cool, cover, and refrigerate. Reheat, covered, in a 350°F. oven until heated through, stirring once or twice, about 45 minutes.)

Stir in the remaining rosemary and lemon zest, and serve.

Grilled Buffalo Steaks with Fiery Chimichurri

Buffalo, or bison meat, is lower in fat, cholesterol, and calories than beef, and because most buffalo are grass fed, their meat has no hormones or antibiotics. It does not taste gamey, but is slightly fuller in flavor than beef. Buffalo meat is available online and at specialty food stores. The available cuts of buffalo meat will vary from store to store. Just make sure that they are not too thick for this recipe. My favorite buffalo steak is the flat-iron. The tart, herbal condiment *chimichurri* is the must-have steak sauce in Argentina, where it pairs perfectly with that country's grass-fed beef. It's equally good on your favorite steak.

YIELD: 4 SERVINGS; 1 CUP CHIMICHURRI

Chimichurri

¼ cup finely chopped shallot

1 bay leaf, preferably fresh,
    torn into 4 pieces

¼ cup extra-virgin olive oil

4 garlic cloves, minced

½ teaspoon crushed red pepper flakes

3 tablespoons red wine vinegar

½ cup finely chopped fresh flat-leaf parsley

1 teaspoon minced fresh thyme

Salt and pepper

Buffalo Steaks

2 teaspoons extra-virgin olive oil

1½ pounds buffalo steaks (¾ inch thick),
    preferably flat-iron or ribeye

Salt and pepper

To make the chimichurri: Combine the shallot and bay leaf in a small bowl. Heat the olive oil in a heavy, small skillet over medium heat. Add the garlic and red pepper flakes and swirl gently until the garlic is tender, about 1 minute (do not brown the garlic). Immediately pour the garlic mixture over the shallot and bay leaf in the bowl. Stir in the vinegar and 1 tablespoon water and let stand until cool. Stir in the parsley and thyme. Season generously with salt and pepper. *(The chimichurri can be prepared up to 2 hours ahead. Cover and let stand at room temperature.)*

To cook the steaks: To fry the steaks, heat the olive oil in a cast iron skillet over medium-high heat. Rub both sides of the steaks generously with salt and pepper. Fry the steaks until browned, turning once, about 6 minutes total for medium-rare doneness. Transfer the steaks to plates, top with a generous spoonful of chimichurri and serve.

Note: *You can also cook these steaks over a grill. Preheat the grill to medium heat and cook as directed above.*

Rabbit with Prunes and Olives

Remember Chicken Marbella from the *Silver Palate Cookbook*? I made (and was served) that dish all the time in the 1980s. The flavor combo of prunes, olives, and oregano is wonderful with chicken and also makes a great braise for rabbit. Although not often eaten in the States, rabbit is enjoyed all over Europe. It's a really clean, lean, super-sustainable meat with a delicate flavor similar to chicken. (When it's boned, I doubt most people can tell the difference!) You can find rabbit at specialty food stores, usually fresh, but sometimes frozen. If not, most butchers will order it for you. Of course, you can always substitute it with chicken. If you make this dish ahead, the flavor will only improve.

YIELD: 4 SERVINGS

2 tablespoons olive oil

1 whole rabbit (about 2¼ to 2½ pounds), cut into 8 pieces

Salt and pepper

1 large onion, chopped

6 garlic cloves, chopped

⅔ cup dry white wine

3 tablespoons red wine vinegar

3 tablespoons chopped fresh oregano or 3 teaspoons dried

2 tablespoons light brown sugar

½ cup pitted prunes

½ cup picholine or other brine-cured green olives

Heat 1 tablespoon of the olive oil in a heavy, large enameled Dutch oven or pot over medium-high heat. Add the rabbit, season with salt and pepper, and cook until golden brown on both sides, about 8 minutes. Transfer the rabbit to a bowl.

Add the remaining 1 tablespoon olive oil, the onion, and garlic to the Dutch oven and cook until well browned, about 5 minutes (the bottom of the pan should be dark brown but not burned). Add the wine and bring to a boil, stirring up all the browned bits from the bottom of the pan (deglazing). Add the vinegar and reduce the heat to low. Return the rabbit to the Dutch oven and add 3 cups water. Add 2 tablespoons of the oregano and the brown sugar. Season with salt and pepper and bring to a simmer. Cover and cook until the rabbit is no longer pink and cooked through, about 30 minutes.

Stir in the prunes and olives and simmer, partially covered, until the rabbit and prunes are very tender, about 15 minutes. *(Can be prepared to this point up to 2 days ahead. Cool, cover, and refrigerate. Return to a simmer.)*

Transfer the rabbit to a serving dish. Boil the liquid in the Dutch oven until it has thickened and reduced to sauce consistency, about 5 minutes. Season the sauce with salt and pepper to taste and spoon over the rabbit. Sprinkle with the remaining 1 tablespoon oregano and serve.

Picholine olives are small green olives from the south of France with a nutty flavor and crunchy texture.

Citrus Grilled Sausages with Green Onions

Sausages are great for spur-of-the moment entertaining. So many markets feature top quality, in-house sausages. A quick stop to buy an interesting selection of links (my favorites are French garlic and Portuguese linguiça), a loaf or two of bread, and some vegetables to grill, and you've got a feast! Grilling the sausages with lemon and orange wedges lends a light citrus flavor that complements any variety of sausage.

YIELD: 6 TO 8 SERVINGS

2 bunches green onions, trimmed
Olive oil
12 sausages (about 3 pounds)
2 oranges, quartered
2 lemons, quartered
Additional orange and lemon wedges, optional

Preheat the grill to medium heat.

Brush the green onions lightly with olive oil and grill until they are just lightly charred, about 2 minutes. Remove from the grill. Place the sausages on the grill and arrange the oranges and lemons around them. Grill, turning the sausages and citrus, until they are browned and the sausages are cooked through, about 8 minutes.

Transfer the sausages and citrus to a platter, squeezing the juices from the grilled oranges and lemons over the sausages. Cut the green onions into thirds and toss gently with the sausages. Garnish with fresh orange and lemon wedges and serve.

Roasted Fennel and Carrots

Roasting brings out the sweetness of carrots and fennel, and the addition of toasted fennel seeds intensifies the licorice flavor in this winning combo. Serve it with roast poultry or fish or as a starter with a crumble of goat cheese.

YIELD: 6 TO 8 SERVINGS

1 teaspoon fennel seeds
1 teaspoon kosher salt
3 tablespoons extra-virgin olive oil, plus more for brushing
2 fennel bulbs, halved and sliced
1 pound baby carrots, tops removed and scrubbed

Toast the fennel seeds in a heavy, small skillet over medium-high heat until fragrant, about 2 minutes. Transfer to a small mortar and pestle or spice mill and coarsely grind with the kosher salt.

Position one rack in the top third and one rack in the bottom third of the oven and preheat to 400°F. Brush two heavy, large, rimmed baking sheets with olive oil.

Toss the fennel in a large bowl with 1½ tablespoons of the olive oil. Transfer the fennel to one prepared baking sheet, spreading evenly. Toss the carrots with the remaining 1½ tablespoons olive oil in the same bowl. Transfer the carrots to the second baking sheet and spread out evenly. Sprinkle the fennel and carrots lightly with the fennel salt.

Roast the carrots and fennel until they are tender and beginning to brown, about 15 to 18 minutes, stirring and rotating the position in the oven once. Season both with the remaining fennel salt and transfer to a platter. Serve warm or at room temperature.

Broccoli with Garbanzo Beans and Lemon

I serve this broccoli dish with simple grilled fish or chicken or as a light vegetarian entrée with good bread.

YIELD: 6 SERVINGS

2 large broccoli heads

Salt

2 tablespoons extra-virgin olive oil

3 green onions, finely sliced

3 garlic cloves, minced

1 (15-ounce) can garbanzo beans, drained

1 scant teaspoon grated lemon zest

½ teaspoon paprika

2 tablespoons fresh lemon juice

Pepper

Cut the broccoli into 1- to 2-inch florets. Peel and trim the stems and cut into ½-inch pieces (you should have about 7 cups).

Bring ½ cup water to a boil in a heavy, large skillet over medium-high heat. Add the broccoli to the skillet and season lightly with salt. Cover and cook until the broccoli is just crisp-tender and the water just evaporates, 3 to 4 minutes. Transfer the broccoli to a serving dish.

Add the olive oil to the same skillet (do not wash). Add two-thirds of the green onions and the garlic and sauté until fragrant, about 1 minute. Add the garbanzo beans and sauté until they are golden brown, 4 to 5 minutes.

Stir in the lemon zest and paprika. Return the broccoli to the skillet, sprinkle with lemon juice, and cook until the broccoli is heated though, about 2 minutes. Sprinkle with the remaining green onions and season with salt and pepper. Return to the serving dish and serve.

Golden and Sweet Potato Gratin

This pure and simply flavored gratin is a good addition to holiday meals. If you like cheese on your gratin, sprinkle the potatoes with 1 cup freshly grated Parmesan or 2 cups grated Gruyère cheese after adding the cream. If you don't care for sweet potatoes, use an additional 1½ pounds Yukon gold potatoes in their place.

YIELD: 8 TO 10 SERVINGS

6 tablespoons unsalted butter, at room temperature

2 cups milk

3 garlic cloves, pressed

2 teaspoons kosher salt

1 tablespoon fresh thyme leaves

½ teaspoon pepper

⅛ teaspoon grated nutmeg

2¼ pounds Yukon gold potatoes, well scrubbed

1½ pounds dark-skinned, dark-fleshed sweet potatoes, peeled

1 cup heavy cream

Preheat the oven to 400°F. Spread 2 tablespoons of the butter over the bottom and sides of a 13 x 11-inch baking dish.

Combine the milk, garlic, salt, thyme, pepper, and nutmeg in a heavy, medium-sized saucepan and bring just to a boil.

Thinly slice the potatoes and the sweet potatoes and place them in the prepared dish. Pour the hot milk mixture over the potatoes. Dot the top with 2 tablespoons of the butter. Cover the dish tightly with aluminum foil and bake until the potatoes are tender and the milk is almost completely absorbed, 35 to 40 minutes. (*Can be prepared to this point up to 1 day ahead. Cool and refrigerate.*)

Meanwhile bring the cream to a boil in a small saucepan. Remove the foil from the baking dish and pour the cream over the potatoes. Dot the top with the remaining 2 tablespoons butter and continue baking uncovered until the cream is very thick and the top of the gratin is golden brown, about 30 to 35 minutes. Cool slightly and serve.

Oven-Roasted Frites with Herbes de Provence

You won't miss the extra fat or fuss of deep-fried French fries (*frites*) when you make this oven-roasted version. These are wonderful served with Chicken Fricassee with Mustard and Marjoram (page 166) or a pan-fried steak. Herbes de Provence is a dried herb blend popular in Southern France. It's usually a mix of basil, thyme, rosemary, savory, marjoram, and bay leaves. My favorite blend is one that contains lavender—check the label or look for the little purple blossoms.

YIELD: 2 TO 4 SERVINGS

2 tablespoons olive oil
1 pound large baking potatoes
½ teaspoon crumbled Herbes de Provence
Fleur de sel
Pepper

Preheat the oven to 400°F. Brush a heavy, large baking sheet with olive oil.

Cut the potatoes into strips that are 3-inches long and ⅓-inch thick and toss them in a large bowl with the olive oil. Spread the potatoes in a single layer on the prepared baking sheet. Bake until the potatoes are golden brown, crisp on the edges, and tender inside, about 35 minutes, stirring three times.

Sprinkle the fries with the herbes de Provence and fleur de sel. Season with pepper, toss well, and serve.

Sautéed Bell Peppers and Golden Raisins with Baby Spinach

This colorful dish is a wonderful accompaniment to roast meats. Because it can be served warm or at room temperature, it's a great addition to a party buffet. You can substitute yellow or orange peppers, if desired.

YIELD: 8 TO 10 SERVINGS

¼ cup plus 1 tablespoon extra-virgin olive oil
6 red bell peppers, cut into strips
⅔ cup golden raisins
2 teaspoons fennel seeds
3 tablespoons balsamic vinegar
Salt and pepper
8 cups (about 6 ounces) baby spinach leaves
Seasalt

Heat ¼ cup of the olive oil in a very large skillet over medium-high heat. Add the peppers and sauté until slightly softened, about 7 minutes.

Add the raisins and fennel seeds, and cook until the peppers are soft, about 5 minutes. Stir in 2 tablespoons of the vinegar and season with salt and pepper.

Meanwhile toss the spinach with the remaining olive oil and vinegar in a large shallow bowl. Season to taste with salt. Spoon the pepper-raisin mixture over the spinach and serve.

Roasted Baby Artichokes

Baby artichokes are fully mature artichokes that have not formed the fuzzy "chokes" that need to be removed from larger artichokes. The babies grow on the same plant as the larger artichokes but stay small because they are closer to the ground under the shade of the leaves. With just a bit of trimming, the entire artichoke is edible. Use artichokes that are 3 inches long or smaller. Serve these with any roast or as an appetizer with an extra drizzle of good olive oil and lemon juice.

YIELD: 4 TO 6 SERVINGS

2 tablespoons fresh lemon juice
2 pounds baby artichokes
2 tablespoons extra-virgin olive oil, plus more for brushing
Salt and pepper

Fill a bowl with cold water and add the lemon juice. Peel back the outer leaves of each artichoke until the exposed leaves are tender and pale green. Trim off the tips and stems and cut the artichokes in half. Place the artichokes in the lemon water. (*Can be prepared to this point several hours ahead.*)

Preheat the oven to 400°F.

Brush a large-rimmed baking sheet with olive oil.

Drain the artichokes and pat them dry. Return the artichokes to the bowl, add the oil, and toss. Transfer the artichokes to the prepared sheet, and sprinkle with salt and pepper.

Roast the artichokes until they are tender when pierced, stirring once, about 20 minutes. Serve warm or at room temperature.

Grilled Ratatouille

Ratatouille is the traditional vegetable stew from Provence. I like to make this version on the grill and serve it with grilled meats. The recipe makes a lot, but whatever doesn't get eaten at dinner makes a good lunch with some crumbled feta cheese in the following days. Pearl tomatoes are about the size of a golf ball. Every summer, I usually end up with a tomato plant that produces lots of very small tomatoes. You can also find the miniature fruit at the farmers' market and at some super markets.

YIELD: 8 TO 10 SERVINGS

1 ½ pounds Japanese eggplants (about 5), cut into quarters

1 pound zucchini, cut in half lengthwise

¾ pound pearl tomatoes or cherry tomatoes

1 red bell pepper, thickly sliced

1 green bell pepper, thickly sliced

1 red onion, cut crosswise into ½-inch slices

3 tablespoons extra-virgin olive oil, plus more for brushing vegetables

Salt and pepper

½ cup mixed chopped fresh herbs (such as basil, cilantro, marjoram, and thyme)

3 garlic cloves, pressed

½ teaspoon lavender blossoms, crumbled, optional

Prepare the grill to medium heat.

Brush the eggplant, zucchini, tomatoes, peppers, and onions lightly with olive oil. Season with salt and pepper.

Grill the vegetables on all sides until they are browned and tender, about 5 minutes for the eggplant and onion, about 4 minutes for the zucchini and bell peppers, and 2 minutes for the tomatoes. Transfer the vegetables to a large baking pan and let them cool to room temperature.

Whisk 3 tablespoons of the olive oil, the herbs, garlic, and lavender together in a large bowl. Add the tomatoes. Coarsely chop the remaining vegetables and transfer them to the bowl. Season with salt and pepper and mix well.

Serve the ratatouille warm or at room temperature. *(Can be prepared up to 2 days ahead. Bring to room temperature before serving.)*

Do you have a grill basket?

I picked up a 12-inch-square, 3-inch-deep perforated metal grill basket at a summer clearance sale and discovered that I enjoyed using it to make grilled veggies. You can get them at barbecue and convenience stores in the summer. To make the ratatouille in a grill basket, cut the eggplant and zucchini into 3/4-inch cubes, cut the peppers into 3/4-inch pieces, and coarsely chop the onion. Toss the vegetables with enough olive oil to coat lightly. Grill the eggplant, zucchini, and tomatoes each separately, stirring occasionally until tender (see cooking times at left). Grill the onion in the basket, stirring occasionally, until it begins to become tender, about 2 minutes. Add the peppers to the onion and continue grilling until the onions and peppers are tender, about 4 minutes. Proceed with the rest of the recipe as directed.

Brussels Sprouts with Marjoram and Pine Nuts

Even people who claim to not like Brussels sprouts have eaten this festive dish contentedly. There is something about the richness of the pine nuts and cream, and the slightly mentholated herb flavor of the marjoram that tempers the strong cabbagey flavor of the sprouts.

YIELD: 6 TO 8 SERVINGS

3 tablespoons unsalted butter
⅔ cup pine nuts
1½ pounds Brussels sprouts, halved
2 large shallots, minced
Salt
1½ tablespoons chopped fresh marjoram
⅓ cup heavy cream
Pepper

Melt 1 tablespoon of the butter in a heavy, large skillet over medium heat. Add the pine nuts and stir until golden, about 3 minutes. Transfer the pine nuts to a small bowl.

Melt the remaining 2 tablespoons butter in the same skillet over medium heat. Add the Brussels sprouts and shallots and stir until coated, about 1 minute. Add 1 cup water and sprinkle with salt. Cover and simmer until the sprouts are almost tender, about 7 minutes.

Uncover and simmer until the water evaporates, about 5 minutes. Stir in 1 tablespoon marjoram, then the cream. Simmer until the sprouts are coated with cream, stirring frequently, about 4 minutes. Season with salt and pepper. *(Can be prepared to this point up to 1 day ahead. Cover and chill. Stir over medium heat to reheat.)*

Gently stir in half the pine nuts. Transfer the Brussels sprouts to a serving dish. Sprinkle with the remaining pine nuts and marjoram, and serve.

Swiss Chard with Morel Mushrooms and Shallots

Morels are dark brown wild mushrooms with spongy, honeycombed, cone-shaped caps. Their slightly smoky, nutty, and earthy flavor really complements chard. Morels are in season from April to June, which happens to be when the chard I grow is plentiful. Morels are usually available at farmers' markets and specialty food stores. Don't hesitate to enjoy plentiful chard sautéed with or without the mushrooms. This spectacular side dish goes really well served with chicken or fish.

YIELD: 6 SERVINGS

2 bunches Swiss chard (about 20 large leaves), ribs removed
3 tablespoons extra-virgin olive oil
2 ounces fresh morel mushrooms
¼ cup minced shallot
Salt and pepper

Stack half the chard leaves and roll them up lengthwise into a cylinder. Slice the leaves crosswise into ½-inch-thick slices. Repeat with the remaining chard (you should have about 10 cups).

Heat the oil in a heavy, large skillet over medium heat. Add the mushrooms and shallot, and season lightly with salt. Sauté until the mushrooms are tender, about 5 minutes. Add the chard and stir to coat. Cover and cook until the chard wilts, about 4 minutes. Season with pepper and transfer to a serving dish.

Asparagus and Peas with Green Garlic

Green garlic is to garlic what green onions are to onions, so the fresh, tender garlic completes this spring vegetable duo. This dish would be lovely served with salmon, lamb chops, or cheese ravioli.

YIELD: 4 SERVINGS

1 tablespoon extra-virgin olive oil

¾ pound asparagus, cut into 3-inch pieces

½ pound Chinese or sugar snap peas, stemmed

2 tablespoons thinly sliced green garlic or 1 large garlic clove, minced

Salt

½ teaspoon grated lemon zest

Heat the olive oil in a heavy, large skillet over medium-high heat. Add the asparagus, peas, and garlic, and stir until coated. Sprinkle with salt and add ¼ cup water. Bring to a boil, cover, and cook until the vegetables are almost cooked and the water is almost evaporated, about 4 minutes.

Add the lemon zest and sauté until the vegetables are tender and the water evaporates, about 1 minute longer. Transfer to a platter and serve.

To prep asparagus, gently bend each spear until it snaps. The spear will break at the point where the asparagus is tough.

Black Beans with Orange and Chipotle

I like black beans that are a dark inky black, so I don't pre-soak the beans. Black beans that are soaked in one batch of water, drained, rinsed, and cooked in a fresh batch of water turn out a sad, gray color. A long, slow simmer with a touch of orange and bay and a hint of smokiness from bacon fat and chipotle make these creamy beans main-course worthy. You can serve the beans as is or sprinkle them with crumbled *queso seco* or feta and chopped fresh cilantro. Simmer the beans an extra 10 minutes or so and you'll have thick beans suitable for filling a burrito.

YIELD: 6 CUPS, ABOUT 6 SERVINGS

¼ cup bacon fat or olive oil
1 large onion, chopped
4 garlic cloves, chopped
1 pound dry black beans, rinsed
3 bay leaves, preferably fresh
12-inch curl orange zest (¾- to 1-inch thick)
1 teaspoon minced canned chipotle chile en adobo
Salt

Heat the bacon fat in a heavy, medium-sized Dutch oven or pot over medium heat. Add the onion and garlic, and sauté until tender, about 8 minutes.

Stir in the beans then add 8 cups water, the bay leaves, and orange zest. Bring the beans to a simmer. Skim any foam from the top of the beans. Partially cover the pot and gently simmer the beans over low heat until they are very tender, stirring frequently, about 1½ hours.

Stir in the chipotle chile and season with salt. Uncover and simmer until creamy, about 15 to 20 minutes. (*Can be prepared 3 days ahead and refrigerated or frozen for up to 1 month.*)

Couscous with Currants, Barberries, and Mint

A staple of North African cuisine, couscous is granular semolina that is traditionally served with stewed meats. Packaged precooked couscous is available in Middle Eastern markets and large supermarkets. Dried barberries are a little peculiar—they resemble small red raisins and are very sour. I first tasted barberries in pilaf at a Persian restaurant and was instantly smitten by their tannic, sweet-tart flavor and ruby-like appearance. You can purchase barberries, called *zereshk* in Persian, at a Middle Eastern or Persian market or substitute chopped dried sour cherries. You can also leave them out—the couscous has plenty of flavor without their unique touch. Dried currants, sometimes called Zante currants, taste like small, strongly flavored raisins. Unfortunately, they're getting harder to find—get them where you buy the barberries or use chopped raisins.

YIELD: 4 TO 6 SERVINGS

3 tablespoons extra-virgin olive oil

2 garlic cloves, pressed

1 teaspoon salt

1 teaspoon turmeric

2 cups couscous

3 green onions, thinly sliced

⅓ cup pine nuts, toasted

⅓ cup currants

¼ cup barberries, optional

¼ cup chopped fresh mint

¼ cup fresh orange juice

2 tablespoons chopped flat-leaf parsley

1 teaspoon grated orange zest

Salt and pepper

photo on page 171

Combine the olive oil, garlic, salt, turmeric, and 2½ cups water in a heavy, medium-sized saucepan and bring to a boil. Remove the pan from the heat and stir in the couscous. Cover and let stand for 5 minutes.

Fluff the couscous with a fork and transfer it to a large bowl. Cool slightly.

Stir in the green onions, pine nuts, currants, barberries, mint, orange juice, parsley, and orange zest. Season with salt and pepper to taste. *(Can be prepared 1 day ahead. Cover and refrigerate. Bring to room temperature before serving.)*

This is an incredibly versatile dish. You could make it a main course by adding diced cooked chicken and serving it on a bed of greens. Here are some other ingredients that would be great to add in addition to, or in place of the additions listed above.

Toasted chopped pistachios
Chopped dried apricots
Chopped fresh cilantro
Chopped fresh dill
Crumbled feta cheese

Lemon Risotto

This versatile risotto can be served as a side dish—it's delicious served with seafood—or as a main course with steamed artichokes or grilled asparagus. I use Meyer lemons, but regular lemons are good too. Although the simplicity of the lemon and fresh parsley is appealing, adding 1 tablespoon minced fresh thyme leaves and 3 ounces chopped prosciutto (along with the onion) is also great. Short-grained Arborio rice is essential for creating the creamy texture desired in risotto. Find it at Italian markets and in the imported foods section of some supermarkets.

YIELD: 6 SERVINGS

3 tablespoons extra-virgin olive oil
1 large onion, finely chopped
1¾ cups Arborio rice
1 cup dry white wine
4 to 5 cups chicken broth or water
2 tablespoons fresh lemon juice
1 teaspoon grated lemon zest
½ teaspoon kosher salt
¾ cup freshly grated Parmesan cheese
2 tablespoons finely chopped flat-leaf parsley
Salt and pepper

My lazy risotto technique: *Traditionally, when making risotto, broth is added in half-cup increments and stirred until the rice absorbs the broth before adding the next bit of broth. I have found that adding the broth all at once and stirring frequently instead of constantly results in an equally creamy texture and frees me to make other preparations in the kitchen.*

Heat the olive oil in a heavy, large saucepan over medium heat. Add the onion and sauté until very tender, about 10 minutes.

Add the rice and stir until translucent, about 2 minutes. Add the wine and stir until it is absorbed, about 2 minutes. Stir in 4 cups of the broth, the lemon juice, lemon zest, and salt. Simmer, stirring frequently, until the rice is tender and creamy, about 20 minutes.

Stir in the Parmesan cheese and parsley and season with salt and pepper. Add enough of the remaining broth to thin the risotto to a creamy consistency if necessary. Serve immediately.

Bay Leaf-Scented Rice Pilaf

Basmati translates as "queen of fragrance" in Hindi. The rice has a long grain, a fine texture, and a nutty perfume. I like to use California or Texas organic basmati in this versatile pilaf that can be served with Indian, Middle Eastern, Southwestern, *and* American food.

YIELD: 6 SERVINGS

2 tablespoons unsalted butter

1 very large shallot or small onion, finely chopped

1½ cups basmati or other long-grain white rice

1 teaspoon coriander seeds

2½ cups chicken broth

½ teaspoon kosher salt

3 fresh bay leaves

2 tablespoons chopped fresh cilantro or flat-leaf parsley

Melt the butter in a heavy, large saucepan over medium heat. Add the shallot and sauté until it is very tender, about 5 minutes. Add the rice and coriander seeds and stir for 2 minutes. Add the broth, salt, and bay leaves. Bring the mixture just to a simmer. Cover and simmer over low heat until all the liquid is absorbed and the rice is tender, about 20 minutes.

Fluff the rice with a fork and transfer to a serving dish. Sprinkle with cilantro and serve.

Creamy Polenta

Polenta is basically cornmeal mush with a pretty Italian name. It's a staple in Northern Italy. For the best flavor and creamiest texture, use good-quality, coarsely milled polenta or grits. Serve with the Braised Lamb Shanks on page 210 for a hearty and comforting meal.

YIELD: ABOUT 6 TO 8 SERVINGS

3 tablespoons unsalted butter
1½ teaspoons salt
1½ cups polenta (not quick-cooking) or yellow cornmeal
⅔ cup freshly grated Parmesan cheese
Pepper

Combine 6 cups water, the butter, and salt in a heavy, large saucepan. Bring to a boil, then whisk in the polenta in a thin stream. Reduce the heat to medium and whisk for 1 minute. Reduce the heat to low. Cover and simmer the polenta, until thick and creamy, stirring occasionally, about 40 minutes.

Stir in the Parmesan cheese and season with pepper to taste. (*Can be made 20 minutes ahead and kept covered at room temperature*).

Leftover polenta?

After dinner, transfer any leftover polenta to an oiled baking pan and form 1/2- to 3/4-inch-thick round. Cover and refrigerate overnight. Cut the chilled polenta into wedges. Heat a thin layer of olive oil in a heavy, large skillet or griddle over medium-high heat. Fry the wedges until they are golden brown on both sides, about 3 minutes per side. Sprinkle with freshly grated Parmesan cheese and serve as an appetizer or side dish.

DESSERTS AND SWEETS

Meyer Lemon Pudding Cake

I ordered *budino* at a fashionable restaurant and was delighted to learn that the dessert was an old-fashioned pudding cake. This dessert, by any name, forms a spongy cake layer on top with a light custard on bottom. It can be both homey and upscale. This recipe makes perfect use of sweet Meyer lemons, although tart tangerines work nicely too. I provide directions for making this a tangerine cake in the note that follows the recipe. Because the skin of both fruits is thin and soft, you will need a Microplane® zester to grate it. Serve sliced strawberries with the lemon cake and sweetened raspberries with the tangerine cake. For a more elegant presentation, bake the cakes in individual custard cups or ramekins. (Eight ⅔-cup custard cups or ramekins bake for 30 minutes.)

YIELD: 6 TO 8 SERVINGS

4 eggs, separated
1 cup sugar
1 tablespoon grated Meyer lemon zest
¼ cup unbleached all-purpose flour
3 tablespoons unsalted butter, melted
¼ teaspoon salt
1½ cups buttermilk
½ cup Meyer lemon juice
Hot water

Preheat the oven to 350°F. Generously butter an 8 x 8-inch baking dish or a 5-cup soufflé dish.

Using a standing mixer, beat the egg whites with ¼ cup of the sugar until medium-stiff peaks form. Transfer the egg whites to a large bowl. Using the mixer (no need to wash the mixer bowl), beat the egg yolks with the remaining ¾ cup sugar and the lemon zest until the mixture is very thick and pale, about 3 minutes. Beat in the flour, butter, and salt, then the buttermilk and lemon juice. Gently stir one-quarter of the egg whites into the yolk mixture. Fold in the remaining whites. Pour the batter into the prepared dish.

Put the dish in a baking pan and add enough hot water to the baking pan so it comes halfway up the sides of the batter in the dish. Place the baking pan in the oven and bake until the cake is just golden brown and slightly springy to the touch, about 45 minutes. Serve warm or chilled.

Variation: *To make tangerine pudding cake, follow the recipe above, substitute tangerine zest for lemon zest and 1 cup tangerine juice for the lemon juice, and use only 1 cup buttermilk.*

Beaumes-de-Venise Cake

I read about this cake long ago in a French Provencial cookbook. *Gateau de Beaumes de Venise aux Raisins*. The title alone conjured memories of farm-style desserts enjoyed in Europe and set my mouth watering. I followed the recipe and was so disappointed in the dense, dry, and lackluster result—what a waste of pricey wine, and worse, where was my *gâteau*?! I immediately set out to replicate the tender wine-flavored, fruit-accented dessert of my dreams. After several attempts, I ended up with this treat. Apricots with sweet Riesling, raspberries with sweet Marsala, and figs with Sauternes are all excellent variations. The aroma that perfumes the house while baking this cake is heavenly. Serve it with a little crème fraîche.

YIELD: 8 TO 10 SERVINGS

¼ cup extra-virgin olive oil, plus more for brushing

1½ cups unbleached all-purpose flour

1 teaspoon baking powder

1 teaspoon salt

¼ teaspoon baking soda

1 cup plus 2 tablespoons sugar

5 tablespoons unsalted butter, at room temperature

2 eggs

1 teaspoon grated lemon or orange zest

1 cup Beaumes-de-Venise, Muscat, or other sweet wine

2 cups grapes, raspberries, apricot quarters, or small figs, cut in half

Preheat the oven to 400°F. Brush a 10-inch springform pan with olive oil. Line the pan with an 11-inch round of parchment paper and brush the parchment with olive oil.

Whisk the flour, baking powder, salt, and baking soda together in a medium-sized bowl.

Whisk 1 cup of the sugar, 4 tablespoons of the butter, and the ¼ cup olive oil in a large bowl until the mixture is well blended and light. Whisk in the eggs and lemon zest. Add the flour mixture alternately with the wine in three additions each, whisking just until smooth after each addition. Transfer the batter to the prepared pan and smooth the top. Sprinkle the grapes over the batter.

Bake the cake until the top is set, about 20 minutes. Dot the top of the cake with the remaining tablespoon of butter; sprinkle with the remaining 2 tablespoons sugar. Bake until the cake is golden and a tester inserted into the center comes out clean, 15 to 20 minutes.

Let the cake cool slightly. Release the pan sides. Slide the cake off the bottom of the pan and onto a platter. Serve slightly warm or at room temperature.

Layered Chocolate Birthday Cake

This impressive cake is deceptively simple—in fact, I developed the recipe so my daughters could bake it for *my* birthday. It's perfect with scoops of vanilla ice cream. For scrumptious results, use chocolate that is between 54 and 61 percent cacao (pure chocolate).

YIELD: 12 TO 16 SERVINGS

Cake

2¾ cups unbleached all-purpose flour

1 teaspoon baking soda

1 teaspoon salt

12 ounces bittersweet chocolate, broken into pieces

½ pound (2 sticks) unsalted butter

2 eggs

2 cups sugar

2 teaspoons vanilla extract

Frosting

12 ounces bittersweet chocolate, chopped or broken into 1-inch pieces

6 tablespoons unsalted butter

⅓ cup sugar

1¼ cups heavy cream

¼ teaspoon salt

1½ teaspoons vanilla

To make the cake: Preheat the oven to 350°F.

Butter three 9-inch round cake pans with 1½-inch or higher sides. Line the bottoms of the pans with parchment. Butter and flour the parchment and sides of the pan.

Whisk the flour, baking soda, and salt together in a medium-sized bowl.

Combine 2 cups water, the chocolate, and butter in a heavy, medium-sized saucepan over medium heat. Stir the mixture occasionally until the chocolate and butter melt and the mixture is smooth, about 5 minutes.

Meanwhile, whisk the eggs, sugar, and vanilla together in a large bowl. Whisk in the melted chocolate mixture, then the flour mixture. Divide the batter evenly into the prepared pans. Bake until the cakes are just slightly firm when touched and a tester inserted into the center comes out clean, about 25 minutes.

Cool the cakes in the pans for 15 minutes. Run small a sharp knife around the edge of each pan. Invert the cakes onto cooling racks, remove the pans and parchment paper, and let the cakes cool completely.

To make the frosting: Combine the chocolate and butter in a medium-sized bowl.

Combine ⅓ cup water and the sugar in heavy, medium-sized saucepan over medium-high heat. Cook until the sugar dissolves, about 1 minute. Add the cream and salt and bring to a boil. Remove the saucepan from the heat and pour the hot cream mixture over the chocolate and butter. Let stand for 5 minutes.

Whisk the chocolate mixture until it becomes smooth. Stir in the vanilla. Let the frosting stand, stirring occasionally, at room temperature until it is just spreadable, about 1 hour.

To assemble the cake: Place one cake layer on a plate and frost the top with ½ cup of frosting. Top with a second layer of cake and spread with ½ cup of frosting. Place the remaining cake layer atop the frosting. Frost the top and sides of the cake with the remaining frosting. *(Can be prepared up to 1 day ahead. Cover with a cake dome and keep at cool room temperature.)*

꙳

You can also use this batter and frosting to make about 2½ dozen cupcakes. Bake them for about 15 minutes.

Easy Banana Cream Pie

Imagine whipping up a cream pie in about an hour. The easy no-roll, no-chill crust has the texture of a cookie. I add a thin layer of chocolate, but if you're a banana pie purist you can leave it out. The pie recipes in this book all use a standard 9-inch pie dish or pan with 1½-inch high sides and a ½-inch rim. The rim is important because it supports the pie crust edge. You can use either a glass or metal dish. I prefer glass because I can peak at the bottom to make sure the crust is properly baked.

YIELD: ONE 9-INCH PIE

Crust

1½ cups unbleached all-purpose flour

¼ cup sugar

½ teaspoon salt

¼ pound plus 3 tablespoons
    unsalted butter, melted

3 ounces bittersweet chocolate,
    finely chopped

Filling

2⅓ cups milk

1 vanilla bean, split in half lengthwise

5 egg yolks

½ cup plus 2 tablespoons sugar

¼ cup cornstarch

2 tablespoons dark rum

2 small or 1½ large bananas, sliced

1 cup heavy cream, chilled

Chocolate shavings, optional

Additional banana slices, optional

To make the crust: Preheat the oven to 350°F. Butter a 9-inch Pyrex or glass pie dish.

Combine the flour, sugar, and salt in a medium-sized bowl. Add the butter and stir with a fork until moist clumps form. Press the dough evenly onto the bottom and up the sides of the prepared dish. Bake the crust until it is golden brown, about 20 minutes.

Remove the crust from the oven and sprinkle it with chocolate. Let it stand until the chocolate melts, about 5 minutes. Using the back of a spoon, carefully spread the chocolate over the crust. Chill or freeze the crust until the chocolate is set, about 30 minutes in the refrigerator or 10 minutes in the freezer.

To make the filling: Bring the milk and vanilla bean to a simmer in a heavy, medium-sized saucepan over medium heat.

Whisk the egg yolks, 1/2 cup of the sugar, and the cornstarch together in a large bowl. Gradually whisk the hot milk into the egg mixture. Return the mixture to the saucepan and whisk over medium-high heat until the custard thickens and boils, about 3 minutes. Remove from the heat and whisk in the rum. Cool the custard to room temperature.

Stir the custard until smooth; remove the vanilla bean. Spoon half the custard into the piecrust. Arrange the banana slices over the custard. Top with the remaining custard. Chill until set, about 2 hours. (*Can be prepared to this point up to 1 day ahead. Cover with plastic wrap and refrigerate.*)

Whip the cream with the remaining 2 tablespoons sugar to soft peaks. Spread the whipped cream decoratively over the pie. Garnish the pie with chocolate shavings and additional banana slices.

To make chocolate shavings, set a large chunk of bittersweet chocolate in a warm place to soften (not melt). Working over a sheet of waxed paper, firmly grasp the chocolate in one hand. Using a vegetable peeler, carefully shave curls of chocolate onto the waxed paper. Carefully lift the edges of the paper and slide the curls and shavings onto the pie.

Blackberry Pie

If I had to choose only one pie to enjoy for the rest of my life, it would be a blackberry pie. I love it so much, I have tried several times to cultivate blackberries in my yard—which leads my Oregon relatives, who are plagued with the berries, to question my sanity! Blackberry pie is great when it's made with freshly picked berries (use less sugar), market berries, and especially frozen berries. You can use the crust recipe for any double-crust fruit pie.

YIELD: ONE 9-INCH PIE

Crust

2⅓ cups unbleached all-purpose flour

1 teaspoon sugar

1 teaspoon salt

¼ pound (1 stick) unsalted butter, chilled and cut into ½-inch cubes

½ cup vegetable shortening, frozen solid and cut into ½-inch cubes

4 to 5 tablespoons ice water

Filling

6 cups fresh blackberries (about 22 ounces) or 2 pounds frozen, thawed and drained well

¾ to 1 cup sugar

¼ cup unbleached all-purpose flour

To make the crust: Combine the flour, sugar, and salt in the bowl of a food processor and pulse to blend. Add the butter and shortening and pulse until the mixture resembles coarse meal. Transfer the dough to a medium-sized bowl and add 4 tablespoons of the ice water. Stir with a fork just until moist clumps form, adding the remaining tablespoon of ice water if necessary to moisten. Gather the dough into two even balls. Flatten the balls into disks, wrap them in plastic, and chill for 30 minutes. *(The dough can be made ahead. Refrigerate for up to 4 days or freeze for 2 weeks. Let frozen dough thaw in the refrigerator overnight and let refrigerated dough soften slightly at room temperature before rolling.)*

Position a rack in the bottom third of the oven and preheat to 400°F.

To make the filling: Gently mix the filling ingredients together in a large bowl.

To assemble the pie: Roll one dough disk out on a lightly floured surface to a 12-inch round. Transfer the dough to a 9-inch glass pie dish. Spoon the filling into the crust. Roll the second disk out on a lightly floured surface to a 12-inch round. Drape the crust over the filling. Press the overhanging top and bottom crusts together, then fold the edge under to be even with edge of the pie dish. Crimp the edges decoratively. Cut a 2-inch "x" in the center of the top crust.

Bake the pie on a rimmed baking sheet until the crust is golden and the filling bubbles thickly in the center, about 1 hour.

To make the piecrust without a food processor: Combine the flour, sugar, and salt in a medium-sized bowl. Add the butter and shortening and rub them into the flour with your fingertips until a coarse meal forms, then proceed with the recipe as written.

Apple Cinnamon Crumb Pie

All my friends who bake this pie tell me that it is the best apple pie ever. I think it is the perfect pie for both novice and expert bakers, because it's easy and yields great results. The loose cinnamon crumb topping that's piled on top of the sliced apples bakes in to a crisp-crumbly crust that's hard to ignore.

YIELD: ONE 9-INCH PIE

Crust

1⅓ cups unbleached all-purpose flour

1 teaspoon sugar

½ teaspoon salt

4 tablespoons unsalted butter, chilled and cut into ½-inch cubes

¼ cup vegetable shortening, frozen solid and cut into ½-inch cubes

3 tablespoons ice water

Filling

3¼ pounds Pippin or Granny Smith apples

⅔ cup sugar

2 tablespoons unbleached all-purpose flour

2 tablespoons unsalted butter, melted

1 scant tablespoon cinnamon

1 generous pinch of salt

Topping

1 cup unbleached all-purpose flour

½ cup sugar

¼ cup light brown sugar, firmly packed

1 slightly rounded teaspoon cinnamon

½ teaspoon salt

6 tablespoons unsalted butter, chilled and cut into ½-inch cubes

To make the crust: Combine the flour, sugar, and salt in the bowl of a food processor and pulse to blend. Add the butter and shortening and pulse until the mixture resembles coarse meal. Transfer the dough to a medium-sized bowl and drizzle the ice water over it. Stir with a fork just until moist clumps form. Gather the dough into a ball; flatten the ball into a disk. Wrap the disk in plastic and chill for 30 minutes. Do not wash the food processor bowl.

Position a rack in the bottom third of the oven and preheat it to 400°F.

Roll the dough out on a lightly floured surface to a 12-inch round. Transfer the dough to a 9-inch glass pie dish. Press the dough gently into the dish, turning the edge of the dough under at the edge of the pie dish. Crimp the edges decoratively.

To make the filling: Peel, core, and cut the apples into ¼-inch-thick slices. Mix all of the filling ingredients together in a large bowl.

To make the topping: Combine the flour, sugars, cinnamon, and salt in the bowl of a food processor and pulse to blend. Add the butter and pulse until the mixture resembles wet sand.

To assemble the pie: Stir the filling and spoon it into the crust, mounding the apples in the center. Pack the crumb topping over the apples, covering them completely. Bake the pie on a rimmed baking sheet until the topping is golden, about 40 minutes.

Reduce the oven temperature to 350°F. and continue baking until the apples are tender when pierced with a small sharp knife, about 40 minutes. Serve warm or at room temperature.

Protect That Crust! Often the crust, especially at the edges, bakes before the pie filling cooks properly. In order to keep the crust from burning while waiting for the filling to cook, protect the crust with an aluminum foil collar. Before the edge of the crust becomes too brown, tear off a piece of foil about 3 feet long. Fold it lengthwise into quarters. Wrap the collar around the edge of the pie and secure it by bending it slightly at the edge. Continue baking the pie.

Rose and Orange-Scented Honey-Nut Tart

This rich nut tart with hints of rose, orange, and clove was inspired by the delicate flavor of Persian baklava. The crust is a bit unconventional—it's simply pressed into the tart pan when it's crumbly, so it is very tender and delicate. I like to serve it with honey-sweetened Greek yogurt that is sprinkled with pomegranate seeds.

YIELD: ONE 11-INCH TART

Crust

1¾ cups unbleached all-purpose flour

⅓ cup confectioners' sugar

1 scant teaspoon salt

⅛ teaspoon ground cloves

10 tablespoons (1¼ sticks) unsalted butter, chilled and cut into pieces

1 teaspoon grated orange zest

Filling

1 cup heavy cream

½ cup sugar

¼ cup light brown sugar, firmly packed

¼ cup honey

¾ cup coarsely chopped walnuts, toasted

¾ cup sliced almonds, toasted

¾ cup pistachios, toasted

1½ teaspoons rose water, optional

To make the crust: Butter the bottom of an 11-inch tart pan with a removable bottom. Combine the flour, confectioners' sugar, salt, and cloves in the bowl of a food processor and pulse together to blend. Add the butter and orange zest and pulse until the mixture resembles moist, coarse meal. Transfer the mixture to the prepared pan (it will be crumbly). Press the dough evenly over the bottom and up the sides of the pan. Freeze the crust while preparing the filling.

Position a rack in the bottom third of the oven and preheat it to 425°F.

To make the filling: Bring the cream, both sugars, and the honey to a boil in a heavy medium-sized saucepan over medium-high heat. Continue to boil until the mixture thickens and darkens slightly, about 4 minutes. Remove from the heat and stir in the nuts and rose water. Spoon the filling evenly over the crust.

Bake until the filling is caramel brown and the crust is golden, about 24 minutes. Cool completely. *(Can be prepared up to 2 days ahead. Cover and keep at cool room temperature.)*

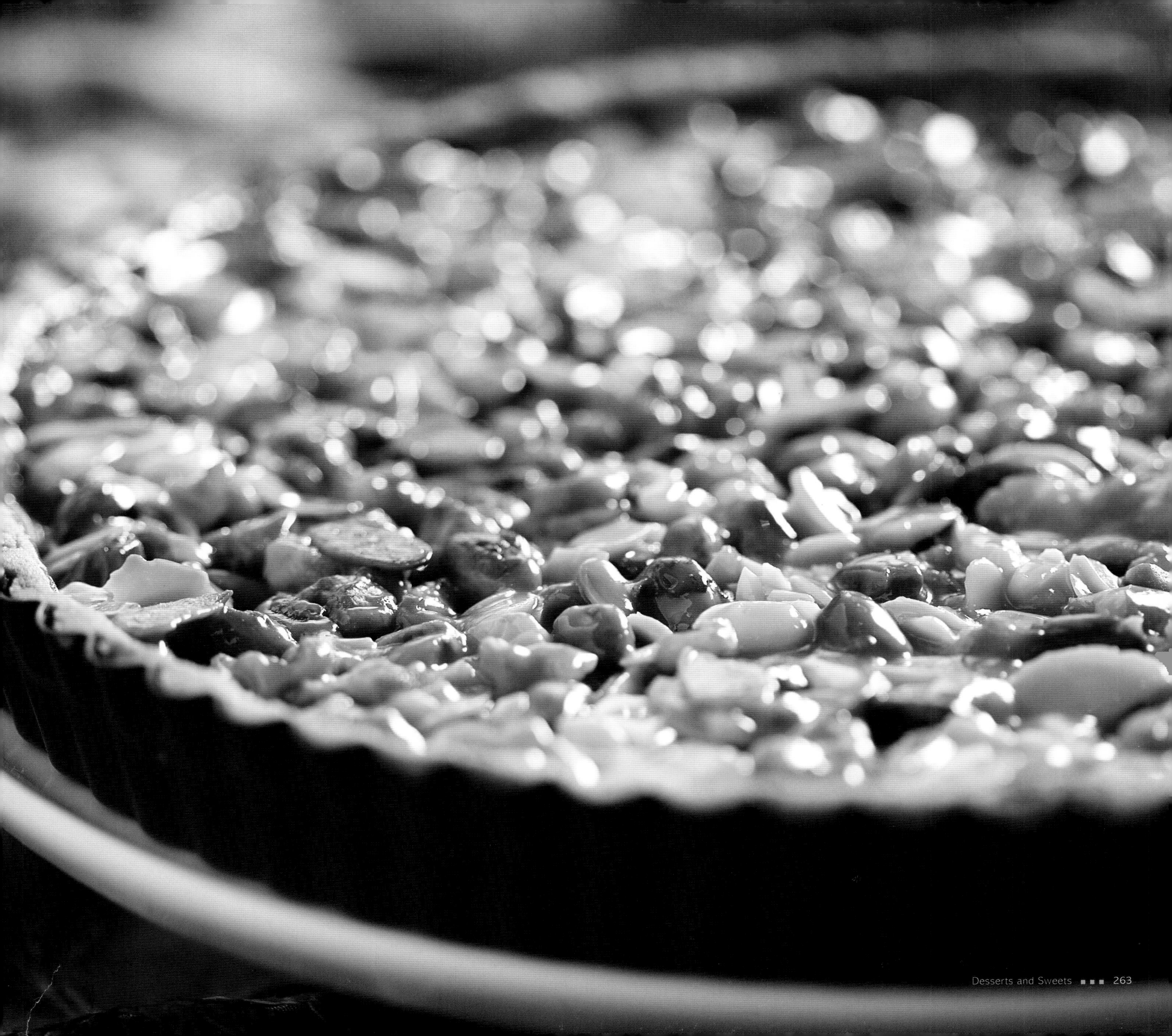

Apricot Crostata with Cornmeal Crust

Crostata is the Italian term for a rustic, free-form tart. The same tart is called a *croustade* in French. I call it either, depending on what kind of dinner I prepare. Cornmeal adds texture and body to the short, buttery crust, and the pretty sprinkling of raw sugar—coarse crystals of unbleached cane sugar—makes it sparkle. By any name, the simple treatment of tree-ripened apricots is delightful.

YIELD: 6 TO 8 SERVINGS

Crust

1¼ cups unbleached all-purpose flour

⅓ cup confectioners' sugar

¼ cup cornmeal

¾ teaspoon salt

10 tablespoons (1¼ sticks) unsalted butter,
    chilled and cut into pieces

2 chilled egg yolks
    (reserve one egg white for the filling)

Filling

1½ pounds ripe apricots (10 to 12),
    halved and pitted

⅓ cup sugar

1 tablespoon unbleached all-purpose flour

1 egg white

2 tablespoons raw sugar

To make the crust: Combine the flour, sugar, cornmeal, and salt in a food processor and pulse to blend. Add the butter and pulse until the mixture resembles coarse meal. Add the egg yolks and pulse until moist clumps form. Gather the dough into a ball, then flatten it into a disk. Wrap the disk in plastic and chill for 20 minutes or up to 4 days.

Preheat the oven to 375°F.

To make the filling: Gently stir the apricots and sugar together in a large bowl until the apricots are lightly coated with sugar. Sprinkle the flour over the apricots and stir gently.

To assemble the crostata: Roll the dough out between 2 sheets of lightly floured parchment paper to form a 13-inch round. Lift the parchment occasionally to keep the dough from sticking. Remove the top sheet of parchment and slide the bottom piece with the dough onto a heavy baking sheet. Arrange the apricot halves over the dough, placing some cut-side up and some cut-side down, leaving a 1½-inch border of dough. Using the parchment as an aid, fold the edges of the dough up over the apricots, pressing gently to seal. Brush the border with the egg white and sprinkle the raw sugar over the egg white. Bake until the crust is golden brown and the juices bubble thickly in the center, about 1 hour.

Cool the crostata slightly. Slide it off the parchment onto a platter and serve warm.

A rimless baking sheet is great to use here as it makes it easy to slide the finished crostata onto a pretty platter. If your apricots seem particularly juicy, line the baking sheet with aluminum foil and turn up the sides. Any juices that run from the tart will be caught before dripping to the bottom of your oven.

Apple-Prune Crisp with Hazelnut-Oat Topping

Apple crisps are fun to make, and brown sugar, prunes, and hazelnuts give this one a bold, wintry quality. If preferred, you can simplify the crisp by omitting the prunes and/or the hazelnuts.

YIELD: 10 SERVINGS

Topping

1 cup light brown sugar, firmly packed

1 cup old-fashioned oats

¾ cup unbleached all-purpose flour

¾ teaspoon salt

¼ pound plus 4 tablespoons (1½ sticks) unsalted butter, chilled and cut into pieces

2 cups hazelnuts, lightly toasted and chopped

Filling

3½ pounds Pippin or Granny Smith apples, peeled, cored, and chopped

1½ cups diced pitted prunes

⅔ cup sugar

⅓ cup light brown sugar, firmly packed

2 tablespoons unbleached all-purpose flour

1 tablespoon cinnamon

Generous grating of fresh nutmeg

Vanilla ice cream, for serving

To make the topping: Combine the brown sugar, oats, flour, and salt in a large bowl. Add the butter and use your fingertips to blend the ingredients together until the mixture is evenly mixed and resembles coarse meal. Stir in the hazelnuts. (*Can be prepared several hours ahead. Cover and refrigerate.*)

Preheat the oven to 375°F. Generously butter a 13 x 9-inch or other shallow, 3-quart baking dish.

To make the filling: Combine all the filling ingredients in a large bowl. Mix well and let stand until the mixture is moist, about 10 minutes.

To assemble the crisp: Transfer the filling to the prepared baking dish. Sprinkle the topping evenly over the filling. Bake until the topping is golden brown and the apples in the center are tender when pierced with a sharp knife, about 1 hour.

Cool slightly and serve warm with vanilla ice cream.

Perfect Chocolate Chip Cookies

Okay, so these chocolate chip cookies are "perfect" because they are made the way I like chocolate chip cookies—just enough salt, crispy on the edges but soft in the center, and studded with walnuts. The cookies are also perfect because I use a cookie scoop to form the dough into evenly rounded half domes of dough that bake into uniform cookies. The cookie scoop looks like an ice cream scoop with a release mechanism—it's really fast and keeps you from eating too much dough.

YIELD: ABOUT 3 DOZEN

1 ½ cups light brown sugar, firmly packed
⅓ cup sugar
½ pound (2 sticks) unsalted butter, at room temperature
2 eggs
1 teaspoon vanilla extract
3 cups unbleached all-purpose flour
1 ½ teaspoons salt
1 teaspoon baking soda
12 ounces chocolate chips
2 cups chopped walnuts

Chocolate chip cookies are best when they are still warm. When I make a batch of dough, I bake a few cookies, then I form the rest of the dough into 2-tablespoon mounds and freeze them on a wax-paper-lined plate. When the dough mounds are firm, I transfer them to a ziplock bag. Whenever I want a cookie, I arrange a few mounds on a cookie sheet, let them stand at room temperature while preheating the oven, then bake.

Preheat the oven to 350°F. Lightly grease two heavy, large baking sheets or line with silicone baking mats.

Using an electric mixer, beat the sugars and the butter together until light. Beat in the eggs and vanilla. Stop the mixer and stir the bottom of the mixture with a rubber spatula. Sprinkle the flour, salt, and baking soda over the mixture and beat well. Stir in the chocolate chips and walnuts.

Working in batches, drop the dough by 2 tablespoonfuls onto the prepared cookie sheets, spacing them 2 inches apart. Bake the cookies, switching the cookie sheets in the oven midway through baking, until they are just beginning to turn golden brown at the edges and the tops appear dry, 12 to 15 minutes. Transfer the cookies to a rack to cool.

Photo on page 268

Chewy Old-Fashioned Fruit Bar Cookies

These not-too-sweet cookies remind me of the lightly spiced fruit bars that you used to be able to find at bakeries. They are great any time of day. You can use any variety of dried fruit and you can add chopped nuts (about 1 cup), too.

YIELD: ABOUT 2 DOZEN

2 cups unbleached all-purpose flour

2 teaspoons baking powder

1 teaspoon ground cinnamon

1 teaspoon freshly grated nutmeg

½ teaspoon ground ginger

½ teaspoon baking soda

½ teaspoon salt

¼ teaspoon ground cloves

¼ pound (1 stick) unsalted butter, at room temperature

1¼ cup light brown sugar, firmly packed

2 eggs

1 cup chopped dried fruit, such as Bing cherries, raisins, or dates

Preheat the oven to 350°F. Line a heavy, large baking sheet with a silicone baking liner or parchment paper.

Whisk the flour, baking powder, cinnamon, nutmeg, ginger, baking soda, salt, and cloves together in a medium-sized bowl.

Using an electric mixer, beat the butter and brown sugar together until smooth and light. Beat in the eggs, then the dry ingredients, then the fruit.

Spoon one-third of the batter onto the prepared baking sheet, about 1 inch from the edge of the baking sheet, and form it into a 9 x 2-inch log. Repeat with the remaining batter, forming two more logs, spaced 3 inches apart. Bake until the tops are slightly cracked and dry in appearance and just beginning to turn golden brown at the edges, 30 to 35 minutes. Move the baking sheet to a cooling rack to cool.

Carefully transfer the logs to a cutting board and slice them crosswise into 2-inch bars. Store the cookies in an airtight container and enjoy within 3 days.

Bittersweet "One-Pot" Brownies

When my daughter Theresa was six, she wondered aloud why the brownies she'd tasted at a playmate's house "had good texture, but no chocolate flavor." When I explained that the offending treats most likely came from a mix, she was puzzled. The brownies we made together were so easy, why would anyone use a mix? I developed this recipe using half a bar of bittersweet chocolate from Trader Joe's, but it's amazing when made with a 9.7-ounce bar of Scharffen Berger Bittersweet chocolate. I've given this recipe (which I've memorized) to many parents.

YIELD: ABOUT 3 DOZEN SMALL BROWNIES

8 to 10 ounces bittersweet chocolate, coarsely chopped

¼ pound plus 2 tablespoons unsalted butter, cut into pieces

1 cup sugar

3 eggs

1 teaspoon vanilla extract

½ teaspoon salt

¾ cup unbleached all-purpose flour

1 cup chopped walnuts or pecans, toasted, optional

Preheat the oven to 350°F. Butter a 9 x 9-inch metal pan.

Melt the chocolate and butter in a heavy, large saucepan over low heat, stirring frequently until the mixture is melted and smooth. Cool slightly, then stir in the sugar. Whisk in the eggs, vanilla, and salt. Stir in the flour. Add the nuts and transfer the batter to the prepared pan.

Bake until a tester inserted near the center of the brownies comes out with a few moist crumbs attached, 20 to 25 minutes. Cool completely. (*Can be prepared 2 days ahead. Cover with aluminum foil.*) Cut into squares and serve.

Santa Rosa Plum Ice Cream

With so many specialty creameries making delicious ice creams and gelati, it can be hard to justify taking the time to make homemade ice cream. Plum ice cream from homegrown or farmers' market Santa Rosa plums is a true exception. There is nothing quite like this rose-hued, sweet-tart, floral frozen treat.

YIELD: 1 QUART

1 pound (about 10) ripe Santa Rosa plums
2 cups heavy cream
6 egg yolks
1 cup sugar

Combine the whole plums and ¼ cup water in a heavy, medium-sized saucepan. Cover the pan and cook the plums over medium-low heat until the plums are very juicy, about 8 minutes. Uncover and continue cooking the plums, mashing occasionally with a wooden spoon until the plum flesh is very tender and falls from the pits. Cool the plums and remove the pits. Transfer the plums to a blender and purée until smooth (you should have 1 to 1⅓ cups purée).

Bring the cream to a boil in a heavy, medium-sized saucepan.

Meanwhile, beat the egg yolks and sugar together in a medium-sized bowl until well blended. Whisk in the hot cream. Return the custard to the saucepan. Stir, over medium-low heat, until the custard thickens to coat the back of a spoon (do not boil). Immediately pour the custard into a bowl and whisk in the plum purée. Cool the custard completely. (Can be prepared to this point up to 1 day ahead. Cover and refrigerate.)

Process the custard in an ice cream maker according to the manufacturer's instructions. Transfer to a container. Cover and freeze until firm. (The ice cream can be prepared 1 week ahead.)

Blood Orange Granita with Vanilla Ice Cream

This is like a sophisticated 50/50 bar or creamsicle. The granita can be served on its own for a lighter dessert. It can also be made with Valencia oranges. I love the perfume of the orange flower water, but the granita is still fantastic without it.

YIELD: 4 SERVINGS

¼ cup sugar
½ teaspoon blood orange zest
1¼ cups fresh blood orange juice
⅛ teaspoon orange-flower water
Vanilla ice cream, for serving
4 blood orange slices, optional

Using your fingers, rub the sugar and orange zest together in medium-sized bowl, so the oils from orange zest are released. Add the orange juice and stir until the sugar dissolves. Stir in the orange-flower water. Pour the mixture into an 8½ x 5-inch loaf pan.

Freeze the granita until it is slushy, about 1 hour, then stir it with a fork. Repeat the freezing/stirring process one or two more times until it is firm. (*Can be made to this point up to 1 week ahead, keep covered and frozen.*)

Using a fork or a grapefruit spoon, scrape the surface of the granita, creating icy flakes. Working quickly, spoon the granita into each of 4 bowls. Place 1 scoop of vanilla ice cream over the granita. Garnish with slices of blood orange and serve.

Orange-Flower Water

Orange-flower water is a distillation of bitter orange blossoms and water. It's a popular addition to desserts in the Middle East. My favorite brand, with the truest taste and fragrance, is made by Cortas, a Lebanese company. You can find it at Middle Eastern markets for around $2.

Buttermilk and Vanilla Bean Panna Cotta

I love the cold silkiness of panna cotta, which translates as "cooked cream." Similar in texture to custard, this Italian classic is set with gelatin instead of eggs. It takes only minutes to prepare and is so adaptable. I serve it in the spring with sliced strawberries; in the summer with fresh plums, apricots, or berries; in the fall with spiced, stewed figs; and in the winter with puréed soft persimmons. You can play with the richness of this dessert—for a lighter, low-fat version, use half-and-half or milk instead of cream, or for something truly decadent, substitute crème fraîche for all or part of the buttermilk.

YIELD: 6 TO 8 SERVINGS

1 envelope unflavored gelatin
2 cups heavy cream
1 vanilla bean, split in half lengthwise
½ cup sugar
2 cups buttermilk, chilled

Measure 2 tablespoons water in a small bowl and add the gelatin. Let stand 5 minutes for the gelatin to soften.

Place 1 cup of the cream in a heavy, medium-sized saucepan. Scrape the seeds from the vanilla bean and add them to the cream along with the pod. Bring the mixture to a simmer. Add the softened gelatin and the sugar and stir until the gelatin and sugar dissolve. Remove from the heat and stir in the remaining 1 cup cream and the buttermilk. Pour into desired mold, glasses, or ramekins (see sidebar). Chill until firm, about 6 hours. (*Can be prepared up to 3 days ahead; cover with plastic.*)

Most often, panna cotta is served unmolded from ramekins on dessert dishes. For large parties, when I'm serving more than one dessert, I like to set the custard in little 2-ounce glasses found in sets of four at the 99 Cent Store. But my favorite is spooning the panna cotta into small dishes from a beautiful, one-of-a-kind pot; that way people can eat as much or as little they like. My friend Selma Morrow, an associate food editor at Bon Appétit *magazine, brings elegant wine glasses of panna cotta to parties. She manages this trick by buying a set of stemmed glasses that come in a protective, partitioned cardboard box. She chills the panna cotta in the glasses until they set, then places the desserts in their box—ready for transport.*

Meyer Lemon Scones

These scones are a lemony, bright addition to any breakfast, brunch, or tea. They also make delicious strawberry shortcakes—just split them in half horizontally and fill with lightly sweetened sliced strawberries and whipped cream.

YIELD: ABOUT 16 SCONES

2 Meyer lemons (see note)

½ cup sugar

2 cups unbleached all-purpose flour

2 teaspoons baking powder

½ teaspoon baking soda

¾ teaspoon salt

¼ pound (1 stick) unsalted butter, chilled and cut into pieces

¼ cup buttermilk, chilled

¾ cup confectioners' sugar

Preheat the oven to 400°F.

Using a Microplane® peeler, remove the zest from the lemons. Squeeze the juice from lemons and set aside.

Using a food processor, process the sugar and lemon zest to release oils from zest. Add the flour, baking powder, baking soda, and salt, and pulse, scraping down the sides of the processor. Add the butter and pulse to blend, until the mixture resembles coarse meal.

In a small bowl, combine the buttermilk and 2 tablespoons of the reserved lemon juice. Pour the buttermilk mixture into the flour mixture in the food processor, and pulse until the dough just forms.

Transfer the dough to a lightly floured surface and knead just to combine. Pat the dough out to a ¾-inch-thick round. Cut the dough into 2-inch rounds using a floured cookie cutter. Gather the scraps, pat them down again, and cut more scones. Transfer the scones to a heavy, large baking sheet, spacing them evenly.

Bake until the scones are just golden, 12 to 15 minutes. Transfer the scones to a rack and cool.

Stir the confectioners' sugar and 4 teaspoons of the lemon juice together in a small bowl. Drizzle the lemon icing decoratively over the scones and cool.

If Meyer lemons are out of season or unavailable, substitute small Eureka lemons.

Savory Bread Pudding with Sage and White Cheddar

I like the simplicity of this dish—it's good with bacon or breakfast sausages. It you like, you can add 6 ounces of cubed Black Forest ham, cooked sausage, or bacon to the pudding.

YIELD: 12 SERVINGS

1 pound loaf rustic or sourdough bread

3 tablespoons extra-virgin olive oil

2 garlic cloves, pressed

2 tablespoons unsalted butter

1 large onion, finely chopped

⅓ cup chopped fresh sage

8 large eggs

2 cups heavy cream

1½ cups milk

1 teaspoon kosher salt

1 teaspoon pepper

2½ cups grated white Cheddar cheese, lightly packed

Preheat the oven to 375°F.

Cut the bottom crust and short ends off the bread and discard. Cut the remaining bread into 1-inch cubes (you should have 10 cups, lightly packed).

Stir the oil and garlic together in a very large bowl. Add the bread cubes and toss to coat. Transfer the bread to a large rimmed baking sheet. Bake the cubes until they are golden brown and lightly crunchy, stirring occasionally, about 20 minutes.

Meanwhile, melt the butter in a heavy, medium-sized skillet over medium heat. Add the onion and sauté until it is translucent, about 8 minutes. Add the sage and stir until it turns dark green and fragrant, about 2 minutes. Let the mixture cool.

Generously butter a 13 x 9 x 2-inch baking dish. In the same bowl used for the bread, beat together the eggs, cream, milk, salt, and pepper. Stir in the onion-sage mixture and 2 cups of the cheese. Add the bread cubes and stir to coat. Transfer the mixture to the prepared dish and let stand for 20 minutes. (Can be prepared to this point up to 1 day ahead. Cover loosely with plastic wrap and refrigerate overnight.)

Sprinkle the pudding with the remaining ½ cup cheese. Bake until set and the top is golden, 50 minutes to 1 hour.

Pecan-Cinnamon Sticky Buns

These sticky buns are tender, nutty, delicious, and very easy to make. I just stir the dough together quickly before going bed, and in the morning I roll it out and form the buns—the dough is never kneaded and the first rise happens overnight.

YIELD: 8 LARGE BUNS

Dough

¼ cup lukewarm water

1 teaspoon active dry yeast

4 tablespoons unsalted butter, plus more for pan

¾ cup cold milk

¼ cup sugar

1 teaspoon kosher salt

1 egg

½ cup white whole wheat flour

2¼ cups unbleached all-purpose flour

Filling and Topping

1½ cups light brown sugar, firmly packed

1½ cups pecans, toasted and chopped

2 teaspoons ground cinnamon

¼ teaspoon salt

¼ pound (1 stick) unsalted butter, melted

To make the dough: Combine the water and yeast in a large bowl and let stand until the yeast dissolves, about 5 minutes. Melt the butter in a small saucepan over medium heat. Remove from the heat and immediately stir in the milk. Cool to room temperature. Add the butter mixture to the yeast mixture. Whisk in the sugar and salt, then the egg. Using a wooden spoon, stir in the whole wheat flour. Gradually add the all-purpose flour, stirring until the dough becomes smooth but very sticky. Generously butter another large bowl. Using a rubber spatula, transfer the dough to the prepared bowl. Cover the bowl with plastic and refrigerate overnight.

To make the filling and topping: Generously butter a 13 x 9-inch Pyrex or glass baking dish. Combine the brown sugar, pecans, cinnamon, and salt in a medium-sized bowl. Add the butter and mix well.

To assemble the buns: Remove the dough from the refrigerator. Using a rubber spatula, transfer the dough to a floured surface (do not punch it down). Lightly sprinkle the dough with flour and roll it out to a 10 x 13-inch rectangle. Sprinkle the dough with 1 cup of the filling, leaving a ½-inch border on all sides. Beginning at one long side, roll up the dough, jellyroll style. Cut the dough in half crosswise, then cut each half into 4 even slices, making 8 buns.

Stir 3 tablespoons water into the remaining topping and spread it evenly over the bottom of the prepared baking dish. Place the rounds, cut side down and evenly spaced, atop the topping mixture in the dish—a row of three, a row of two, and a row of three (the rounds will not cover the topping completely).

Cover the dish loosely with plastic wrap. Let the buns rise in a warm, draft-free area until they are puffed and have increased slightly in volume, about 1 to 1½ hours.

Position a rack in the lower third of the oven and preheat it to 400°F.

Bake the buns for 10 minutes. Reduce the heat to 375°F. Bake until the buns are golden brown, about 20 minutes. Carefully turn the buns out onto a large, rimless baking sheet and cool slightly. Serve warm.

Easy Huevos Rancheros

I like to make these on the rare weekend mornings we get to sleep in. Because I don't usually plan this breakfast (or brunch) ahead, I usually use a little can of Herdez salsa verde. But if you want to go all out, you can make your own salsa with the recipe on the right.

YIELD: 4 SERVINGS

4 corn tortillas
1 tablespoon olive oil, plus more for brushing
2 cups grated mozzarella cheese, lightly packed
1 teaspoon ground cumin
4 eggs
Salt
1 cup salsa verde, canned or homemade
¼ cup chopped fresh cilantro
1 avocado, sliced
Salsa picante (such as Valentina brand), to taste

Preheat the oven to 400°F.

Brush both sides of the tortillas with olive oil and arrange them on a baking sheet. Bake until crisp, about 15 minutes. Remove the tortillas from the oven.

Preheat the broiler.

Sprinkle each tortilla with ¼ cup cheese and ¼ teaspoon cumin and return them to the baking sheet. Broil the tortillas until the cheese melts, about 2 minutes.

Heat 1 tablespoon olive oil in a heavy, large skillet over medium heat. Add the eggs and fry them, just until the whites set, about 2 minutes. Top each tortilla with an egg and season with salt. Sprinkle the eggs with the remaining 1 cup cheese and broil just until the cheese melts (the egg yolks should still be soft), about 3 minutes.

Meanwhile, add the salsa verde to the same skillet and bring it to a simmer. Transfer the egg-topped tortillas to plates. Spoon the salsa verde over the eggs, sprinkle with cilantro, and garnish with avocado slices. Drizzle the eggs with salsa picante and serve.

Salsa Verde

2 poblano chiles
½ pound tomatillos, husked, rinsed, and quartered
1½ cups low-sodium chicken broth
2 large green onions, chopped
1 garlic clove
¼ cup fresh cilantro leaves, firmly packed
Salt and pepper

Char the chiles directly over a gas flame or in the broiler until blackened on all sides. Transfer to a bowl; cover with plastic, allowing them to steam while cooling. Peel, seed, and chop the chiles.

Combine the tomatillos, broth, green onions, and garlic in a medium-sized saucepan. Bring to a boil over medium-high heat. Reduce the heat to medium-low and simmer until the mixture is reduced to 1¾ cups, stirring occasionally, about 15 minutes. Transfer the mixture to a blender. Add the roasted chiles and cilantro and purée until smooth. Season with salt and pepper. (*Can be made 2 days ahead. Transfer to small bowl; cover and chill.*)

Artichoke, Parmesan, and Green Garlic Frittata

I love green garlic—it's regular garlic in the milder "green" stage. You can use both the tender bulb, and the scallion-like stalks. It's available at farmers' markets in the spring, but it is easy to grow your own from store-bought garlic cloves. (To find out how, go to page 24.) Arugula flowers are the small, peppery blossoms plucked from arugula plants just as they end their plant life. Serve this thin, delicate frittata with sliced strawberries for breakfast or brunch. The egg dish also makes a delicious, light supper when paired with a green salad and a glass of chilled rosé.

YIELD: 2 TO 4 SERVINGS

8 baby artichokes or 12-ounces frozen artichoke hearts

2 tablespoons extra-virgin olive oil

¼ cup thinly sliced green garlic or 1 finely chopped garlic clove

Salt

4 eggs, beaten

Pepper

⅓ cup finely grated Parmigiano-Reggiano cheese, packed

Arugula flowers or flat-leaf parsley leaves, for garnish

If you are using fresh artichokes, trim and cut them into ½-inch-thick wedges. Bring the artichokes and water—½ cup for fresh artichokes and ¼ cup for frozen—to boil in a heavy, well-seasoned or nonstick 10-inch skillet over medium-high heat. Drizzle the artichokes with the olive oil, cover, and cook until the water evaporates and the artichokes are just tender, about 6 minutes for fresh and 3 minutes for frozen.

Uncover the pan, add the garlic, and sauté until the garlic and artichokes are tender, about 2 minutes. Reduce the heat to medium and shake the skillet to evenly distribute the artichokes. Season the artichokes with salt.

Preheat the broiler.

Carefully pour the eggs over the artichokes and season with pepper. Cook until the eggs are just set on the bottom, about 3 minutes. Sprinkle the frittata with the cheese and broil until the eggs are just set, about 2 minutes.

Transfer the frittata to a large platter and garnish with arugula flowers or parsley. Serve warm or at room temperature.

Tip: *To prepare baby artichokes, peel back the outer leaves until the artichoke is pale green. Cut off the tip and stem.*

Chunky-Chewy Fruit and Nut Granola

This granola is great with yogurt and fruit. The recipe can be doubled (use two baking sheets) to make a great gift from the kitchen. Depending on the variety of date you use, you may want to measure the dates before pitting. If the dates are the moist variety, like medjools or bari, simply tear them into pieces. Deglet Noor dates are a firmer, dryer variety that can be purchased pitted—and they chop easily. Date nuggets are also suitable.

YIELD: ABOUT 8 CUPS

3 cups rolled (old fashioned) oats
½ cup whole raw almonds
½ cup raw pepitas (pumpkin seeds)
½ cup coarsely chopped pecans or walnuts
¼ cup flaxseed, optional
1 teaspoon ground cinnamon
½ cup light brown sugar, firmly packed
¼ cup honey
¼ cup light molasses, not blackstrap
2 tablespoons grapeseed or vegetable oil
½ teaspoon kosher salt
¾ cup chopped pitted dates
½ cup dried cherries or raisins

Preheat the oven to 325°F. Grease a heavy, large-rimmed baking sheet.

Mix the oats, almonds, pepitas, pecans, flaxseed, and cinnamon in a large bowl.

Combine the brown sugar, honey, molasses, oil, salt, and ¼ cup water in a heavy, medium-sized saucepan over medium heat and cook until the sugar dissolves, about 1 minute. Bring the mixture to a boil, then pour over the oat mixture and mix well. Spread the oat mixture evenly on the prepared baking sheet. Bake until the granola turns golden brown, stirring occasionally with a spatula, about 40 minutes.

Sprinkle the dates and cherries over the granola and stir to combine. Continue baking until brown, stirring once, about 10 minutes longer. Stir the granola and set the baking sheet aside to allow the granola to cool completely. *(Can be prepared up to 1 week ahead. Store in airtight containers.)*

Blueberry Buckwheat Pancakes

I love the nutty flavor of buckwheat pancakes—and this version of the classic is thin and full of berries. Several markets carry frozen, wild blueberries. I always keep a bag in my freezer. Serve these with warm maple syrup.

YIELD: ABOUT 18 (4-INCH) PANCAKES

½ cup whole ground buckwheat flour

½ cup white whole wheat flour

1 tablespoon sugar

¾ teaspoon baking soda

¾ teaspoon salt

2 eggs

1½ cups buttermilk

2 tablespoons unsalted butter, melted

1 cup fresh or frozen wild blueberries

Butter, for cooking

Maple syrup, for serving

Whisk the flours, sugar, baking soda, and salt together in a medium-sized bowl.

In a large bowl, beat the eggs until well blended, then whisk in the buttermilk and butter. Whisk the dry ingredients into the buttermilk mixture; stir in the blueberries.

Preheat a griddle or skillet over medium-high heat. Melt some butter on the griddle, greasing the griddle completely. Spoon about 3 tablespoons of the batter onto the griddle, creating a 4-inch pancake. Repeat with more batter, evenly spacing the pancakes so they aren't too crowded. Cook until a few holes appear on the surface of the pancake and the bottom is well browned, about 3 minutes. Using a spatula, carefully flip the pancakes over. Place a little nob of butter on the top of each pancake and cook until the second sides are golden brown, about 1 minute. Transfer to plates and serve with maple syrup.

Yeast-Raised Whole Wheat Buttermilk Waffles

This recipe is adapted from a recipe Marion Cunningham's *Breakfast Book*. I use buttermilk, less butter, and white whole wheat flour for an equally delicious yet more wholesome waffle. The batter is mixed, for the most part, the night before. The yeast gives the waffles a wonderful flavor and extra-light texture. Because waffles tend to cool quickly, serve them on heated plates with warm syrup. We enjoy these on Sunday mornings, eagerly awaiting them while we read the paper.

YIELD: ABOUT 20 (4-INCH) WAFFLES

Day 1

½ cup lukewarm water

1 package active dry yeast

4 tablespoons unsalted butter

1 cup reduced fat milk

1 cup buttermilk

1 teaspoon sugar

1 teaspoon salt

1 cup white whole wheat flour

1 cup unbleached all-purpose flour

Day 2

2 eggs

½ teaspoon baking soda

4 tablespoons unsalted butter,
  melted, for cooking

Warm maple syrup, for serving

Day 1: Combine the water and yeast in a very large mixing bowl (to accommodate for the rising batter). Let stand until the yeast dissolves, about 5 minutes.

Melt the butter in heavy, medium-sized saucepan. Remove the saucepan from the heat and immediately add the milk and buttermilk (the mixture should be just warm to touch). Add the milk mixture, sugar, and salt to the yeast mixture and mix well to combine. Stir in the flours. Cover the bowl with plastic wrap and let stand at room temperature overnight.

Day 2: Preheat a waffle iron.

Beat the eggs and baking soda into the batter, which will be thin. Brush the waffle iron with melted butter. Spoon some batter onto the waffle iron (the amount will vary depending on the size of the waffle iron). Close the waffle iron and cook until the waffle is golden on both sides, about 4 minutes (the cooking time will vary depending on the waffle iron). Repeat with the remaining batter and melted butter.

Serve immediately with warm maple syrup.

Ruby Grapefruit and Orange Salad with Pomegranate and Mint

This colorful salad looks like a box of jewels. The culinary term for the nude citrus sections is *suprême*. The orange flower water adds an exotic touch, but you can leave it out.

YIELD: 4 TO 6 SERVINGS

2 ruby grapefruit
2 oranges
1 tablespoon honey
⅛ teaspoon orange-flower water, optional
¼ cup pomegranate seeds
2 tablespoons mint leaves

Using a serrated knife, cut the peel and white pith from the grapefruit and oranges. Cut in between the membranes to release the segments. Transfer the segments to a platter. Drizzle them with honey and sprinkle with the orange-flower water. Squeeze the juice from the citrus membranes over the segments. Sprinkle the fruit with the pomegranate seeds and the mint. Serve or cover and chill up to 4 hours.

There are many ways to peel a pomegranate, but here's one that makes the least mess. The juice from a pomegranate can stain fingers, clothes, and surfaces very easily, so I prefer the "mining" technique: Use a sharp knife to cut off the pomegranate's tip (crown) and bottom. Carefully score a circle around the pomegranate, then cut another circle, effectively scoring the pomegranate into quarters. Fill a very large bowl with clean water. Submerge the pomegranate and carefully pull the quarters of the fruit apart, revealing the jewel-like pips beneath. Working under water, use your fingers to release the pips from the white membrane. The pips will sink to the bottom of the bowl and the membrane and skin will float to the surface. Skim off the debris, strain the pips and enjoy!.

Melon
with Lemon Verbena

Lemon verbena, *la verveine* in French, is a popular herb in Provence where it is used to make herb teas, liqueurs, and even soap. The thin, slightly tough, pale green leaves have a delicate lemon aroma and flavor. I like to sprinkle finely sliced leaves of the herb on fresh fruit to add brightness. The best place to find lemon verbena is on the bush at nurseries, but some farmers' market herb stands sell it as well.

YIELD: 4 TO 6 SERVINGS

1 ripe cantaloupe or Tuscan-style melon
1 tablespoon finely sliced lemon verbena leaves

Cut the melon in half and scoop out the seeds. Cut the melon into wedges are use a knife to cut off the rind. Arrange the slices on a platter and sprinkle with the lemon verbena. Let stand at cool room temperature for about 20 minutes before serving, or cover and chill for up to 3 hours.

Tzaziki with Smoked Salmon and Olive Bread

Tzaziki is a Greek cucumber and yogurt sauce, and it stands in for cream cheese in this, my version of bagels and lox. I took this idea from my dear friend Francesca, whose husband happens to be part Greek. She served this combination as part of a late breakfast buffet at the beach.

YIELD: 4 SERVINGS

1 cup Greek yogurt or ⅔ cup plain yogurt
   mixed with ⅓ cup sour cream
1 small garlic clove, pressed
2 Persian cucumbers, quartered and sliced, or 1 cucumber,
   peeled, quartered, seeded, and sliced
1 green onion, sliced
2 tablespoons minced fresh dill
Salt and pepper
4 ounces sliced smoked salmon
1 small loaf black olive bread, sliced
Dill sprigs

Greek yogurt is sometimes called strained yogurt because the whey is strained from the yogurt, resulting in a thick and creamy texture. Fage is an excellent brand, but Trader Joe's also carries it's own good brand. You can strain your own yogurt by lining a strainer with several layers of cheesecloth and setting it over a bowl in the refrigerator overnight.

Combine the yogurt and garlic together in a medium-sized bowl. Add the cucumbers, green onion, and dill. Season lightly with salt and generously with black pepper; mix well. *(Can be prepared to this point up to 3 days ahead. Cover and refrigerate.)*

To serve, transfer the tzaziki to a small bowl and place on a platter with the salmon and bread. Pass, allowing your guests to spoon the tzaziki onto the bread slices, top with a piece of salmon, and garnish with sprigs of dill.

Baked Eggs with Bacon, Aged Gouda, and Chard

I keep my fresh eggs in a pretty basket at room temperature, but for successful baked eggs, be sure to use eggs straight from the refrigerator—using chilled eggs will result in set whites and slightly runny yolks. To see if your eggs are properly cooked, insert a thin, sharp knife into the egg—the white should be set and the yolk runny. Aged gouda has a much sharper, stronger flavor than regular gouda, but if you can't find it, substitute aged cheddar or use a combination of Parmesan and fontina cheeses.

YIELD: 2 SERVINGS

4 thick slices applewood-smoked bacon

6 small leaves Swiss chard (about 5 inches long, without stems)

4 tablespoons grated aged Gouda, packed

2 eggs, chilled

Pepper

2 slices sourdough bread, toasted

Cut the bacon crosswise into ¾-inch-thick pieces and fry it in a heavy, medium-sized skillet over medium heat until crisp, about 5 minutes. Using a slotted spoon, transfer the bacon to a paper towel to drain.

Pour off all of the fat from the skillet, reserving a small amount. Add ¼ cup water to the skillet and return it to medium heat. Add the chard, cover, and cook until the leaves just wilt, about 1 minute. Cool the chard slightly and drain.

Preheat the oven to 375°F.

Brush 2 small (about 1 cup) ramekins with the reserved bacon fat. Place 3 chard leaves in each ramekin, covering the bottom completely and extending about 2-inches up the sides. Sprinkle one-quarter of the bacon into the lined ramekins, dividing evenly. Top each with ½ tablespoon cheese. Crack the eggs into the ramekins and season with pepper. Sprinkle the remaining cheese and bacon over the eggs, dividing evenly. Bake until the cheese melts and the egg whites are set, about 13 minutes.

Using a thin rubber spatula, unmold the eggs onto the toast and serve.

Tunisian "Brik"–Inspired Eggs with Potatoes, Feta, and Harissa

A *brik* is a Tunisian deep-fried pastry with a thin crust and a whole egg in the center. When I want to enjoy the wonderful North African flavors of a brik, but don't want to bother with the pastry or the necessary deep frying, I make this—eggs, potatoes, and feta cheese combined in a skilled dish and served with warm flat bread.

YIELD: 4 SERVINGS

1 pound white- or red-skinned boiling potatoes, quartered

Salt

2 tablespoons extra-virgin olive oil, plus more for brushing

½ teaspoon caraway seeds

½ teaspoon turmeric

Pepper

4 eggs

3 ounces crumbled feta

¼ cup Harissa Drizzle (pages 130-131)

4 (6-inch) round Middle Eastern flatbreads

¼ cup chopped fresh cilantro or flat-leaf parsley

Place the potatoes in a heavy, small saucepan and add enough water to cover. Season the water with salt and bring the potatoes to a simmer. Cook until the potatoes are just tender when pierced with a sharp knife, about 10 minutes. Drain the potatoes, let them cool, and dice them. *(Can be prepared to this point up to 2 days ahead. Refrigerate.)*

Heat the oil in a heavy, large skillet over medium heat. Add the potatoes, caraway seeds, and turmeric and cook until the potatoes begin to brown, about 10 minutes. Season with salt and pepper to taste. Push the potatoes to the edge of the skillet and reduce the heat to low. Crack the eggs into the skillet, spacing evenly. Sprinkle the feta over the eggs and drizzle with the harissa. Cover and cook until the egg whites are set, but the yolks are still soft, about 5 minutes.

Meanwhile brush the flatbreads with olive oil and heat them on a griddle until warm, turning once. Place one flatbread on each of 4 plates. Top the flatbreads with the eggs and potatoes, dividing evenly. Sprinkle with cilantro and serve.

Fresh Ricotta Blintz Casserole with Strawberries

Blintzes are crepes filled with soft cheese. In this recipe, a fresh ricotta filling and a light buttery cake layer create an equally delicious dish with much less fuss. This is a lovely casserole to serve for a brunch—holiday or otherwise. I like to offer it with strawberries in season, but it's also good with a blueberry compote, mixed berries, or any kind of fruit preserves. Fresh ricotta is a sweeter version of ricotta with a shorter shelf life. You can find it at Italian markets and specialty food stores, or substitute whole milk ricotta.

YIELD: 6 TO 8 SERVINGS

Filling

4 ounces cream cheese,
   at room temperature

¼ cup sugar

1 teaspoon grated lemon zest

1 egg

15 ounces fresh whole milk ricotta cheese

Batter

⅔ cup unbleached all-purpose flour

2 teaspoons baking powder

¼ teaspoon salt

¼ pound (1 stick) unsalted butter, melted
   and slightly cooled

2 eggs

⅓ cup sugar

2 tablespoons milk

½ teaspoon vanilla extract

Topping

3 baskets or 1½ pounds strawberries,
   hulled and sliced

2 tablespoon sugar

½ teaspoon grated lemon zest

Confectioners' sugar, for garnish

To make the filling: Combine the cream cheese, sugar, and lemon zest in a large bowl and beat with an electric mixer until smooth. Beat in the egg, then stir in the ricotta. *(Can be prepared to this point up to 1 day ahead. Cover with plastic and refrigerate.)*

To make the batter: Preheat the oven to 325°F. Butter a 13-inch oval baking dish.

In a large measuring cup or bowl, whisk together the flour, baking powder, and salt. Whisk in the butter, then the eggs, sugar, milk, and vanilla. Spread one-third of the batter (about ½ cup) evenly over the bottom of the prepared baking dish. Spoon the filling evenly over the batter. Drop the remaining batter by spoonfuls over the top of the filling, covering completely. Bake until the casserole turns a golden brown and puffs slightly in center, about 50 minutes.

To make the topping: Combine the strawberries, sugar, and lemon zest in a bowl and let stand until the sugar dissolves, about 15 minutes.

Cool the casserole slightly, about 15 minutes. Sprinkle with confectioners' sugar and serve with the strawberry topping.

Apricot Jam

This is a quick-style jam that is not "canned," meaning it is not processed in a water bath. It needs to be refrigerated and should be enjoyed within 2 weeks, but I usually can't keep it around any longer than a weekend. The recipe multiplies easily if you're lucky enough to have an apricot tree.

YIELD: ABOUT 2 CUPS

2½ pounds ripe apricots, halved and pitted
1 cup sugar

Place the apricots in a heavy, large nonreactive saucepan. Cook over medium heat until the apricots reduce by half, about 40 minutes, stirring occasionally. Reduce the heat to low, add the sugar, and stir until the sugar dissolves. Continue cooking, stirring occasionally until the jam thickens slightly and is reduced to 2¼ cups, about 15 minutes. Cool slightly, spoon into jars, and refrigerate.

Hazelnut and Chocolate Crumb Coffee Cake

This incredibly easy cake is moist and tastes perfect for those of us who love a bit of chocolate with our morning coffee. It's also a great afternoon snack and a good lunchbox treat. The cake is also tasty with pecans or walnuts.

YIELD: ONE 9-INCH-SQUARE CAKE

2 cups unbleached all-purpose flour

1 cup light brown sugar, firmly packed

½ cup sugar

¼ pound (1 stick) unsalted butter, at room temperature

¾ teaspoon salt

¾ cup chopped hazelnuts, toasted

3 ounces bittersweet chocolate, finely chopped

1 teaspoon baking soda

1 cup buttermilk

1 egg

½ teaspoon vanilla extract

Preheat the oven to 350°F. Butter a 9-inch-square pan.

Combine the flour, both the sugars, the butter, and salt in a large bowl and beat with an electric mixer until the mixture resembles coarse meal. To make the topping, transfer ¾ cup of the mixture to a medium-sized bowl, stir in the hazelnuts and chocolate, and set aside.

Mix the baking soda into the remaining butter-sugar mixture in the large bowl. Add the buttermilk, egg, and vanilla, and mix just to combine. Transfer the batter to the prepared pan, spreading evenly. Sprinkle the topping evenly over the batter. Bake until the cake is golden brown and a toothpick inserted into the center comes out clean, about 45 minutes. Cool in the pan on a rack. Cut into pieces and serve. (*Can be prepared 2 days ahead. Wrap the pieces individually in plastic wrap and keep in a cool place.*)

Chicken Keeper's Guide

What's the best thing about backyard chickens? Everyone who keeps laying hens has the same answer: the eggs. Fresh eggs are awesome. A side-by-side taste test with even an expensive free-range organic market egg will prove no comparison. It's like comparing apples to oranges. And surprisingly, chickens make great pets—they are easy to care for, amusing, beautiful to look at, and given the chance, are quite sociable. If you have children, raising chickens can be an excellent educational opportunity.

Our backyard chickens lay delicious eggs, their manure composts into a rich soil amendment that helps our vegetables grow, and they eat the bugs that would like to eat our garden. To taste the synthesis of this arrangement in a simple fried egg, tomato, and garden green sandwich is a joy—simple and beautiful. I must point out that while I have tended a backyard flock for about 15 years, I don't consider myself a chicken expert—I'm a chicken enthusiast. I "muddle through," as my Pop would say, and though I may not be doing everything right, my hens seems happy and the eggless months are few. Here are some guidelines for keeping chickens.

. . .

GETTING STARTED

Check with your town, county, or city to see what the rules are about keeping backyard chickens. Generally, you can keep chickens as long as they are 20 feet away from your home and 40 feet away from your neighbor's house. Most importantly, talk to your neighbors. If they like the idea of hearing a little hen music and being treated to a basket of eggs now and then, well, perhaps you can stay ignorant of local ordinances. Chickens can smell if you don't keep your coop tidy or when the ground is moist in the winter, so the distance recommendations should, at the very least, be considered.

Raising chicks is fun and easy. In the beginning, the fluffy little peepers require the most attention, as you will need to keep them warm, clean, dry, well fed, and watered.

Chick Checklist

- Warm draft-free area, perhaps in your garage, laundry room, or kitchen
- Cardboard box with sides that are at least 12 inches high
- Newspaper
- Work light with a 60-watt light bulb
- Small chicken feeder
- Small chicken waterer
- Chicken wire for top of box (so the chicks won't fly out)
- Quick-grow chick food
- Water
- AND CHICKS!

With the exception of the draft-free area and maybe the cardboard box, you can pick up all that you need, including the chicks, at a feed store. Your local feed store is a wealth of information and equipment. Although not exactly local, my favorite nearby feed store is Wes's Pets and Feed in El Monte, California. "Wes" (who isn't really named Wes) almost always has the answers to my questions and he has plenty of charts, books, and visual aids.

Choose a breed of chicken that is known for being a good layer. (There are laying, meat, and dual-purpose breeds.) It is also important to select chickens that are well suited to your climate. My sister, who lives in Santa Fe, New Mexico, requires a breed of hen that can withstand cold winters, whereas I look for chickens that can take the heat. My flock consists of two Plymouth Rock, two Australorps, and five Araucana hens that lay pale blue eggs. Other good layers are Wyandotes and Rhode Island Reds.

How Many?

Chickens are social animals and should never be raised alone. Some stores won't even sell single chicks. When deciding how many chicks to purchase, figure out how large a flock you would like, then factor in the chances of one being a rooster or not surviving. I usually start with five or six chicks. Four hens will lay about 1½ dozen eggs per week in the summer.

Select lively, loud chicks with clean bottoms. At Wes's, they catch the chicks and drop them into a lunch-size brown paper bag with a few holes punched into the sides for air. After the top of the bag is stapled shut, the chicks are ready for their noisy ride home.

Care and Feeding of Chicks

We start baby chicks off in a large cardboard box in the garage. I line the box with layers of newspaper, several sections thick. This way, as the peepers soil the top layer or section of newsprint—which they will do with regularity—I simply roll up the top section, enclosing the debris and exposing the clean layer below. All this is done without having to remove the chicks, food, or water. As the chicks grow and the box dirties too quickly, I move them to a larger box.

To keep the chicks warm, we use a clip-on reflector light from a building supply store with a 60 to 100 watt bulb. Temperature in the

box should be about 90°F. when the chicks are just hatched. The rule of thumb is to decrease the temperature by 5°F. each week (by moving or changing the light bulb) until the temperature reaches 70°F. You can tell if your chicks are too warm if they crowd against the edge of the box, avoid contact with each other, or seem listless. By contrast, the chicks are too cold if they huddle in a tight clump under the heat source.

As I suggested earlier, you'll need to buy a chick feeder and waterer. The feeder is a covered dish with openings that allow the chicks to eat, but prevent them from scratching, roosting, and pooping in the food. The waterer is a small dish that screws onto a water-filled jar. When the jar is inverted, water flows into the dish as needed by the thirsty chicks. You'll also need quick-grow, which is a feed that is formulated especially for baby chicks. I usually buy 20 pounds of it and switch to regular laying mash or pellets when I run out.

When the chicks "feather out"—grow feathers all over—at about 4 weeks and become poults, you can begin to keep them outdoors. We have a three-foot-square cage with a wooden bottom in the chicken yard that we use for the poults first outside home. You can use any cage that does not have a wire floor, as wire will damage their feet. Keep the cage covered at night with a tarp or an old blanket to protect against drafts. We let the chicks out of the cage and into the enclosed chicken yard during the day, and herd them back to the smaller cage for the night. After a while, the chicks begin to roost on the perches, poles, or branches where the hens sleep, in the chicken coop or yard and leave their so-called teenage "digs" behind.

Chicken Coops

Our coop is a 7 x 4-foot shedlike structure with a 5-foot ceiling, a secure door, and wire-covered openings for air. A 3 x 1½-foot nesting box with a nifty hatch opens to the outside for egg collection. Chickens sleep or roost at night on perches, which are poles or tree

branches. Our coop is located in a chicken-wire-enclosed 15 x 20-foot oak-shaded yard. Hens basically need a place to stay dry, find shelter from the wind, shade from the sun, and protection from predators. A custom-built coop, an old playhouse, or even a dog-house can protect a flock, depending on its size.

If predators are not a worry, you can let your hens roam as long as you provide a safe place for them to sleep at night. Chickens will always roost in the same spot, so you can count on them to return to the coop or henhouse in the evening. We once had chickens that roosted in the branches of an oak tree. In the evenings, my husband Martin, the girls, and I would go up our little hill, sometimes with a glass of wine, and sit and enjoy the sight of our hens flying into the oak, and then performing an awkward ballet as they shifted, fell, relaunched, relocated, and settled themselves among the branches as the sun set in the background.

Food and Water for Chickens

Feed your hens commercial feed such as laying mash or pellets that are formulated with the right amount of protein for good egg pro-duction. Chickens need to eat grit—sand and small pebbles—to properly digest food. Chickens that forage will swallow tiny stones and grains of sand and confined hens will get their grit from their feed as most commercial feeds contain it. The feed also supplies the hens with calcium for strong eggshells. Supplement your chickens' diet with garden and kitchen scraps. Whenever we weed the garden, we throw all the weeds to the chickens to eat. They really go crazy for oxalis. In the kitchen, I keep two canisters next to the sink. In one, I put the garbage destined for the compost—such as coffee grounds, onion, garlic scraps, citrus bits, and eggshells. In the other, I put all the fruit, vegetable, and grain scraps, and feed it to the chickens. They happily nibble their way through carrot and potato peels, apple and pear cores, stems from herbs, and their absolute favorites—melon seeds and rinds and corn cobs.

Some chicken keepers treat their chickens as a live roaming com-post pile, giving them everything, including table scraps (convenient if you have little children who don't want to eat the dregs of their cereal or crusty bits of peanut butter and jelly sandwiches). Chickens are omnivores and will eat anything including meat, sour milk, and chicken. Except for the bugs they eat, my chickens are vegetarian.

Chickens can also be left on their own to forage for food in the garden. They will lay fewer eggs, but they we be wild and free. Although picturesque and pastoral, we found that giving chickens complete access to the garden has its drawbacks. Chickens love the same foods that we do, and don't think twice about helping them-selves to your heirloom tomatoes, baby lettuces, and precious berries. They may also deposit eggs in secret places leading to a daily egg hunt. I once discovered 26 eggs underneath the jade tree and aloe tangle on the hill, and that was only because I happened to see the crafty hen emerge from the plants.

Always have a fresh, clean supply of water for your chickens, especially in the summer. We have an automatic waterer that is attached to a hose valve. The water is replenished as the chickens drink. There are more simple waterers available at feed stores, and you can even use a large, shallow bowl if you are willing to clean the debris and dirt that the chickens will kick into the bowl daily.

Roosters?

I am often surprised at how often I explain that no, you don't need a rooster to get eggs. Yes, you do need a rooster if you want fertilized eggs that hatch into chicks, but a hen ovulates, just as a female human does, with or without the presence of a male. I prefer unfer-tilized eggs and keep only hens, even though I do think roosters are gorgeous. Roosters are the showy sex. They are glossy, colorful, proud, but so incessantly loud. Sometimes, after several weeks of nurture, one of my supposed girl-chicks will reveal itself as a rooster with the beginnings of a colorful tail plume and some laughable screeches that are his feeble attempts at a cock-a-doodle-do. Though handsome, they crow all day long, including the predawn hours and on weekend mornings when you (and your neighbors) are trying to sleep in. Still, I'm sorry to see a cockerel go when we trade him in to the feed store for a bag of scratch. The hens, by contrast, seem quite content to have the randy brute gone.

Eggs

Baby chicks will grow into pullets—young hens less than one year old—and begin to lay eggs at five months. The first eggs are "pee-wee" eggs, about 1½ inches long. I usually blow these eggs, keeping the tiny eggshell intact. After feasting on scrambled eggs, I'm left with the cute little eggs to use as decoration. As the hens get older, their eggs get larger.

Sunlight will affect the amount of eggs your hens lay. Egg production is best in the summer when the days are long. Winter brings shorter days and fewer eggs. In January and February, our hens lay infrequently, as little as one egg a week. Large commercial egg producers keep laying hens in artificially lighted coops 24/7 to increase output.

Encourage your hens to lay in a clean spot with convenient access for gathering eggs. Chickens like a bit of privacy when they lay eggs, and they are easily coaxed into using a nesting box—a box that is just a bit larger than a chicken. Line the nesting place with straw or pine pet bedding to make it cleaner and more inviting to the hen. I put a couple of "fake eggs"—one concrete and one stone in the nest to encourage laying and discourage egg pecking.

It's important to have your hens lay eggs in a clean spot because you want the eggs to be as clean as possible. Avoid washing the eggs. Freshly laid eggs have an invisible antibacterial coating called *bloom* that retards spoiling and keeps the eggs from drying out. If there is some dirt or chicken poop on the egg, gently wipe it clean with a damp towel. An egg will keep for about one month in the refrigera-

tor. I've never kept an egg around that long, as we consume them too quickly. I keep the freshly laid eggs in a basket on the counter, and move them to the refrigerator if I don't think the eggs will be used within a couple of days. When it gets really hot, refrigerate eggs to avoid spoilage. If you think an egg might be too old, here's a good way to test it: fill a small, deep bowl with water. Place the suspect egg in the water. If the egg floats to the surface, chuck it—it's most likely rotten.

. . .

I love the pale blue eggs that my hens lay, and although I refer to them as Araucana, they might not be. They could be Ameraucanas or they could be mutts. There are actually breed standards and poultry fanciers, and getting a purebred Araucana or Ameraucana is similar to acquiring an AKC-registered puppy. When purchased as chicks, my birds came from a hatchery that dubbed them "Araucana with American mix." One official-looking Araucana website that I researched claimed haughtily that if your chicks came from a feed store, they're simply "barnyard chickens with the blue egg-laying gene." Regardless of my birds' breeding, they are cute and they're good layers.

. . .

Weird Hen Behavior

If a chicken loses her feathers and begins to look raggedy, don't think of ways to dispose of her (to keep the rest of the brood from being infected) or rush her off to vet for tests—the hen is just molting. Molting occurs when a chicken is about a year old and then happens yearly. It's a six-week process of old feathers falling out and new ones growing in. All chickens do this, but with some it's more noticeable than with others. Hens will not lay eggs while molting.

If a chicken sits on the nest day after day, she has gone broody. The chicken thinks she is incubating the eggs, even when you remove the eggs (quickly, as she will peck at you). Hens will brood, even with unfertile and "fake" eggs. I just keep pushing the brooding hen off her nest until she finally gets the picture or some timing instinct lets her get on with her life.

If it seems like one of your chickens is being picked on, that's because she probably is. Chickens establish a pecking order and the one at the bottom gets bullied. When young chickens are added to older hens, a hierarchy is established. It can resemble gangland at first, but after a few days, the birds get along fine.

Manure

Chicken manure is highly prized by gardeners. It's too "hot" to add directly to the soil in your vegetable and flowerbeds—it's so nutrient rich that it could actually damage plants by burning the root structures. But when composted, chicken droppings make an excellent soil amendment, high in nitrogen, phosphorus, and potassium. You can compost the manure by adding it to your existing compost pile or by raking the manure into a mound and combining it with garden waste, such as grass clippings, leaves, and weeds and letting the lot sit for two to three months with an occasional mixing. Martin likes to brag that he makes the best compost, but I think the hens deserve some of the credit.

Other Pets

Chickens get along well with other animals. We keep our hens with our goat, and they've shared the yard with rabbits too. Depending on the temperament of your dog, your chickens may even become friends with Fido. We had an old, mellow mutt named Francis who never bothered the chickens. There were mornings when I would see Bard, the Bard Plymouth rock chicken, our cat Coco, and Francis all lined up outside the sliding glass doors waiting for breakfast. We now have a wild cattle dog named Moxie, and we keep her away from the hens.

The Avian Flu

According to the Center for Disease Control and Prevention, flocks of chickens in the United States are not considered at risk of contracting avian flu at this time. If influenza A (H5N1) should ever reach our shores, you can protect your flock from disease by keeping them away from the wild birds, such as sparrows, that can spread the virus through their droppings. Achieve this by enclosing the chickens in a fenced yard and wrapping the fence with a nylon mesh to keep small feral birds out. Cover the yard with a roof or netting. Hopefully this is a scenario that will never occur. Remember, you cannot get avian influenza from properly handled and cooked eggs and poultry.

Index